ACHIEVE LEVEL 5

MATHEMATICS Practice Questions

Louise Moore
Series Editor: **Richard Cooper**

RISING STARS

Rising Stars UK Ltd., 22 Grafton Street, London W1S 4EX

www.risingstars-uk.com

All facts are correct at time of going to press.

First published 2003
This edition 2008

First edition written by: Mark Patmore
Educational consultant: Allison Toogood
Project management: Cambridge Publishing Management Ltd.
Project editor: Catherine Burch
Illustrations: Tim Oliver
Design: Neil Adcock
Cover design: Burville-Riley Partnership

British Library Cataloguing in Publication Data
A CIP record for this book is available from the British Library.

ISBN 978-1-84680-279-9

Printed by Craft Print International Ltd, Singapore

Contents

The answers can be found in a pull-out section in the middle of this book.

How to use this book

Level 4 Tricky Bits practice questions

1. A set of warm-up practice questions, organised by topic. Provides practice in all the Level 4 Tricky Bits included in the Achieve Level 5 Maths revision book.

2. Each question has space for the answers, a specific number of marks (like a real National Test question). Answers are included in the middle of the book. Marking guidance is provided.

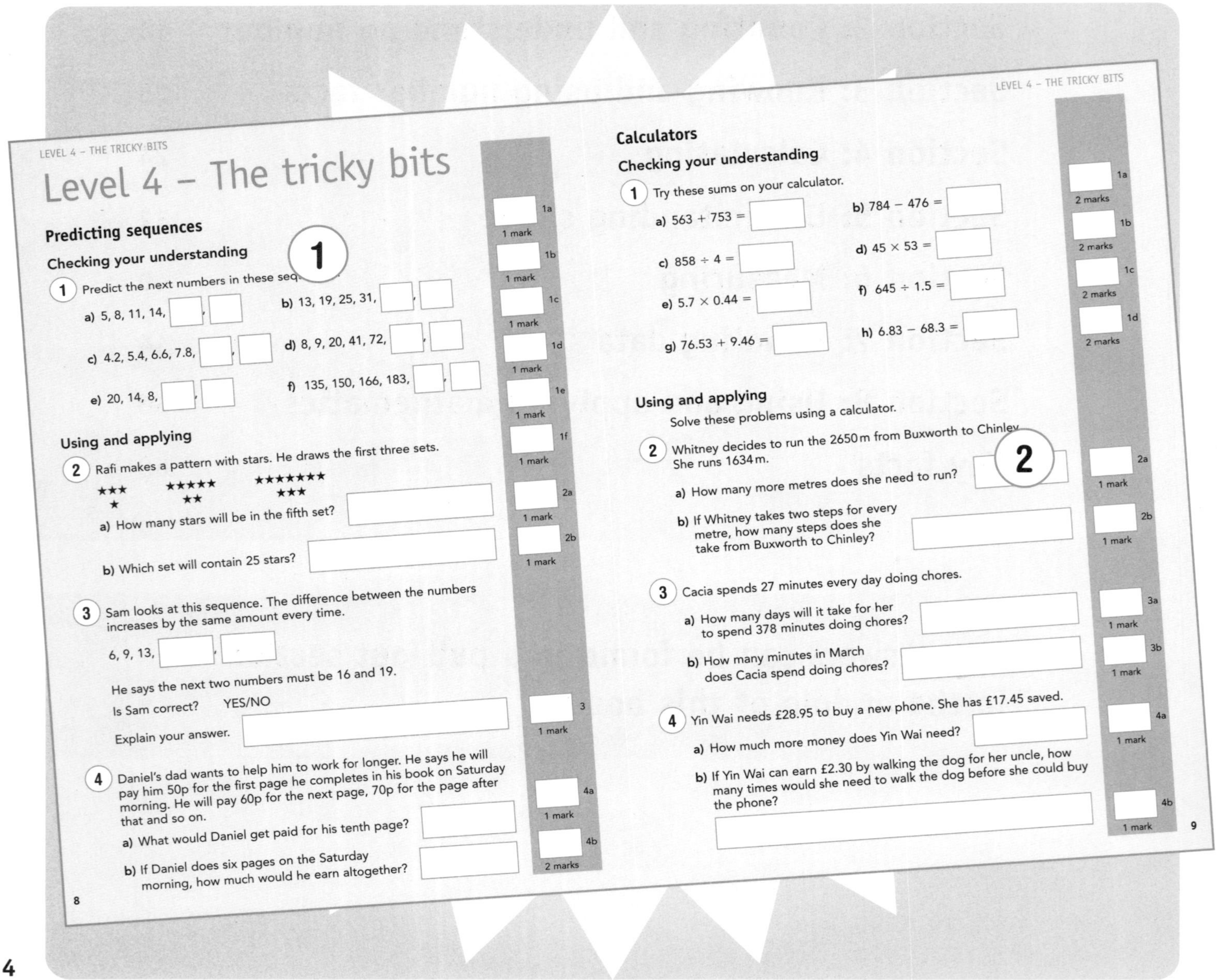

LEVEL 4 – THE TRICKY BITS

Level 4 – The tricky bits

Predicting sequences

Checking your understanding (1)

1 Predict the next numbers in these seq...

a) 5, 8, 11, 14, ___, ___ b) 13, 19, 25, 31, ___, ___

c) 4.2, 5.4, 6.6, 7.8, ___, ___ d) 8, 9, 20, 41, 72, ___, ___

e) 20, 14, 8, ___, ___ f) 135, 150, 166, 183, ___, ___

Using and applying

2 Rafi makes a pattern with stars. He draws the first three sets.

a) How many stars will be in the fifth set?

b) Which set will contain 25 stars?

3 Sam looks at this sequence. The difference between the numbers increases by the same amount every time.

6, 9, 13, ___, ___

He says the next two numbers must be 16 and 19.

Is Sam correct? YES/NO

Explain your answer.

4 Daniel's dad wants to help him to work for longer. He says he will pay him 50p for the first page he completes in his book on Saturday morning. He will pay 60p for the next page, 70p for the page after that and so on.

a) What would Daniel get paid for his tenth page?

b) If Daniel does six pages on the Saturday morning, how much would he earn altogether?

1a 1 mark, 1b 1 mark, 1c 1 mark, 1d 1 mark, 1e 1 mark, 1f 1 mark, 2a 1 mark, 2b 1 mark, 3 1 mark, 4a 1 mark, 4b 2 marks

8

LEVEL 4 – THE TRICKY BITS

Calculators

Checking your understanding

1 Try these sums on your calculator.

a) 563 + 753 = b) 784 – 476 =

c) 858 ÷ 4 = d) 45 × 53 =

e) 5.7 × 0.44 = f) 645 ÷ 1.5 =

g) 76.53 + 9.46 = h) 6.83 – 68.3 =

Using and applying

Solve these problems using a calculator.

2 Whitney decides to run the 2650 m from Buxworth to Chinley. She runs 1634 m. (2)

a) How many more metres does she need to run?

b) If Whitney takes two steps for every metre, how many steps does she take from Buxworth to Chinley?

3 Cacia spends 27 minutes every day doing chores.

a) How many days will it take for her to spend 378 minutes doing chores?

b) How many minutes in March does Cacia spend doing chores?

4 Yin Wai needs £28.95 to buy a new phone. She has £17.45 saved.

a) How much more money does Yin Wai need?

b) If Yin Wai can earn £2.30 by walking the dog for her uncle, how many times would she need to walk the dog before she could buy the phone?

1a 2 marks, 1b 2 marks, 1c 2 marks, 1d 2 marks, 2a 1 mark, 2b 1 mark, 3a 1 mark, 3b 1 mark, 4a 1 mark, 4b 1 mark

9

Topic questions

1. Sets of questions on all the topics you need to cover for the Maths National Tests. Each topic includes some questions on Using and applying mathematics.

2. Each topic matches a section in the Achieve Level 5 Maths revision book.

3. Each question has space for the answers and a specific number of marks (like a real National Test question). Answers are included in the middle of the book.

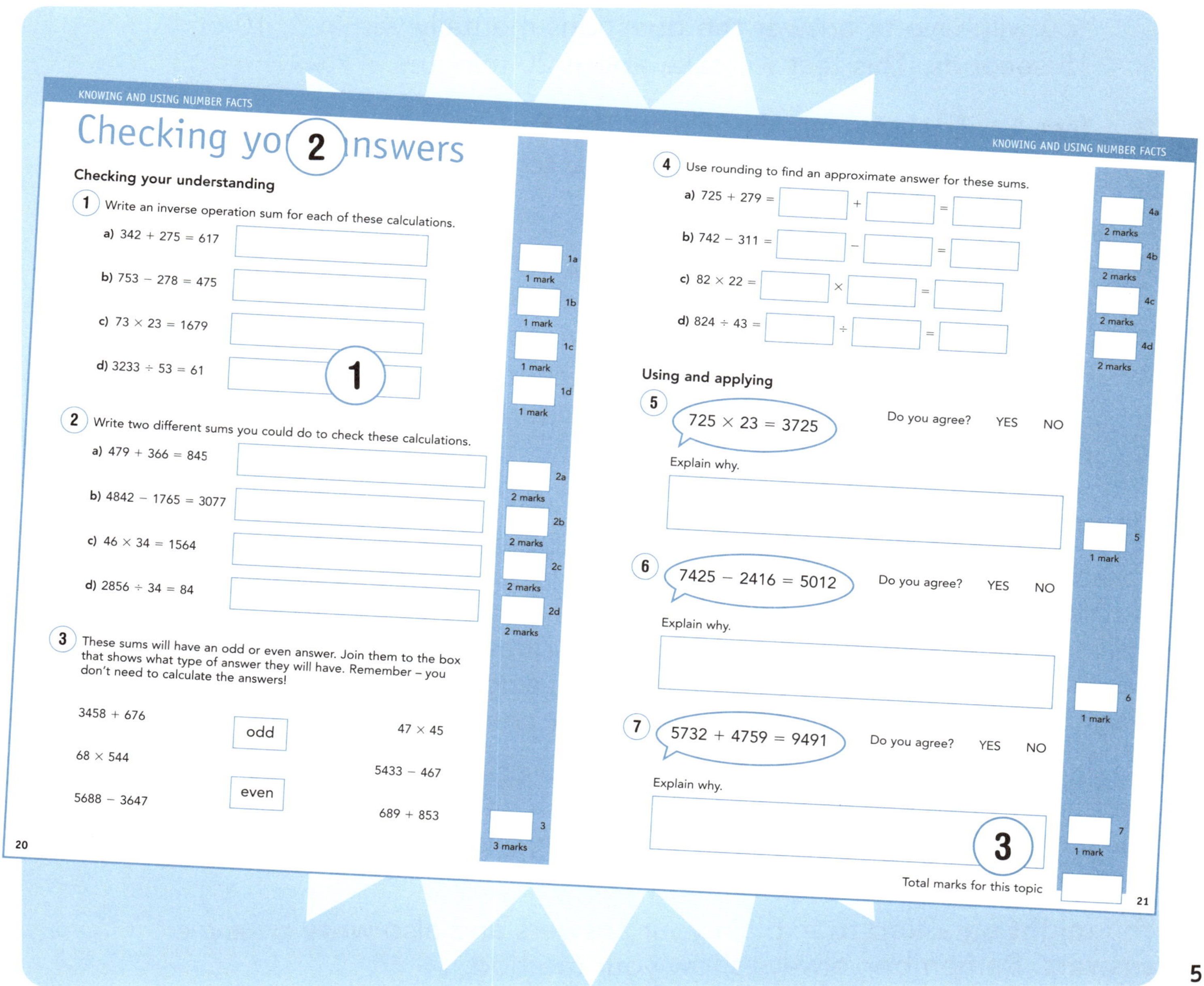

KNOWING AND USING NUMBER FACTS

Checking your answers

Checking your understanding

1 Write an inverse operation sum for each of these calculations.

a) 342 + 275 = 617 (1a, 1 mark)

b) 753 − 278 = 475 (1b, 1 mark)

c) 73 × 23 = 1679 (1c, 1 mark)

d) 3233 ÷ 53 = 61 (1d, 1 mark)

2 Write two different sums you could do to check these calculations.

a) 479 + 366 = 845 (2a, 2 marks)

b) 4842 − 1765 = 3077 (2b, 2 marks)

c) 46 × 34 = 1564 (2c, 2 marks)

d) 2856 ÷ 34 = 84 (2d, 2 marks)

3 These sums will have an odd or even answer. Join them to the box that shows what type of answer they will have. Remember – you don't need to calculate the answers!

3458 + 676 | odd | 47 × 45
68 × 544 | even | 5433 − 467
5688 − 3647 | | 689 + 853

(3, 3 marks)

20

KNOWING AND USING NUMBER FACTS

4 Use rounding to find an approximate answer for these sums.

a) 725 + 279 = ☐ + ☐ = ☐ (4a, 2 marks)

b) 742 − 311 = ☐ − ☐ = ☐ (4b, 2 marks)

c) 82 × 22 = ☐ × ☐ = ☐ (4c, 2 marks)

d) 824 ÷ 43 = ☐ ÷ ☐ = ☐ (4d, 2 marks)

Using and applying

5 725 × 23 = 3725 Do you agree? YES NO
Explain why. (5, 1 mark)

6 7425 − 2416 = 5012 Do you agree? YES NO
Explain why. (6, 1 mark)

7 5732 + 4759 = 9491 Do you agree? YES NO
Explain why. (7, 1 mark)

Total marks for this topic

21

About the National Tests

Key facts

- The Key Stage 2 National Tests take place in the middle of May in Year 6. You will be tested on Maths, English and Science.
- The tests take place in your school and will be marked by examiners – not your teacher!
- You will get your results in July, two months after you take the tests.
- Individual test scores are not made public but a school's combined scores are published in what are commonly known as league tables.

The Maths National Tests

You will take three tests in Maths:

- **Mental Maths Test** – This test will be played to you on an audio CD. You will have to answer the questions mentally within 5, 10 or 15 seconds. This test will take about 20 minutes.
- **Test A** – The non-calculator test. This test requires quick answers on a test paper. You will not be able to use a calculator but should show any working you do.
- **Test B** – This test allows you to use a calculator and includes problems that will take you longer to solve. If you do calculations on the calculator, remember to write down what you did. You might get a mark for the correct method, even if you get the answer wrong. Remember, the calculator is only as a good as the person who uses it!

Using and applying mathematics

There will be more questions testing how you use and apply your mathematical knowledge in different situations. This includes: knowing which is the important information in the questions; how to check your results; describing things mathematically using common symbols and diagrams; and explaining your reasons for conclusions that you make.

Many of the questions include elements of using and applying mathematics but we have also added extra pages with specific questions designed to help you succeed in this new area of testing (pages 50–59).

You might be asked to explain your answers and also write possible answers. Remember, always show your method.

Test techniques

Before the test

1 When you revise, try revising a 'little and often' rather than in long sessions.
2 Learn your multiplication facts up to 10 × 10 so that you can recall them instantly. These are your tools for performing your calculations.
3 Revise with a friend. You can encourage and learn from each other.
4 Get a good night's sleep the night before.
5 Be prepared – bring your own pens and pencils.

During the test

1 Don't rush the first few questions. These tend to be quite straightforward, so don't make any silly mistakes.
2 As you know by now, READ THE QUESTION THEN READ IT AGAIN.
3 If you get stuck, don't linger on the same question – move on! You can come back to it later!
4 Never leave a multiple choice question. Make an educated guess if you really can't work out the answer.
5 Check how many marks a question is worth. Have you 'earned' those marks with your answer?
6 Check your answers. You can use the inverse method or rounding method. Does your answer look correct?
7 Be aware of the time. After 20 minutes, check to see how far you have got.
8 Leave a couple of minutes at the end to read through what you have written.
9 Always show your method. You may get a mark for showing you have gone through the correct procedure even if your answer is wrong.
10 Don't leave any questions unanswered. In the two minutes you have left yourself at the end, make an educated guess at the questions you really couldn't do.

Things to remember

1 If you see a difficult question, take your time, re-read it and have a go!
2 Check every question and every page to be sure you don't miss any!
3 If a question is about measuring, always write in the UNIT OF MEASUREMENT.
4 Don't be afraid to ask a teacher for anything you need, such as tracing paper or a protractor.
5 Write neatly – if you want to change an answer, put a line through it and write beside the answer box.
6 Always double-check your answers.

Level 4 – The tricky bits

Predicting sequences

Checking your understanding

1 Predict the next numbers in these sequences.

a) 5, 8, 11, 14, ☐, ☐ **b)** 13, 19, 25, 31, ☐, ☐

c) 4.2, 5.4, 6.6, 7.8, ☐, ☐ **d)** 8, 9, 20, 41, 72, ☐, ☐

e) 20, 14, 8, ☐, ☐ **f)** 135, 150, 166, 183, ☐, ☐

1a 1 mark
1b 1 mark
1c 1 mark
1d 1 mark
1e 1 mark
1f 1 mark

Using and applying

2 Rafi makes a pattern with stars. He draws the first three sets.

★★★ ★★★★★ ★★★★★★★
★ ★★ ★★★

a) How many stars will be in the fifth set? ☐

2a 1 mark

b) Which set will contain 25 stars? ☐

2b 1 mark

3 Sam looks at this sequence. The difference between the numbers increases by the same amount every time.

6, 9, 13, ☐, ☐

He says the next two numbers must be 16 and 19.

Is Sam correct? YES/NO

Explain your answer. ☐

3 1 mark

4 Daniel's dad wants to help him to work for longer. He says he will pay him 50p for the first page he completes in his book on Saturday morning. He will pay 60p for the next page, 70p for the page after that and so on.

a) What would Daniel get paid for his tenth page? ☐

4a 1 mark

b) If Daniel does six pages on the Saturday morning, how much would he earn altogether? ☐

4b 2 marks

Calculators

Checking your understanding

1 Try these sums on your calculator.

a) $563 + 753 =$ ☐ b) $784 - 476 =$ ☐

c) $858 \div 4 =$ ☐ d) $45 \times 53 =$ ☐

e) $5.7 \times 0.44 =$ ☐ f) $645 \div 1.5 =$ ☐

g) $76.53 + 9.46 =$ ☐ h) $6.83 - 68.3 =$ ☐

1a 2 marks
1b 2 marks
1c 2 marks
1d 2 marks

Using and applying

Solve these problems using a calculator.

2 Whitney decides to run the 2650 m from Buxworth to Chinley. She runs 1634 m.

a) How many more metres does she need to run? ☐

2a 1 mark

b) If Whitney takes two steps for every metre, how many steps does she take from Buxworth to Chinley? ☐

2b 1 mark

3 Cacia spends 27 minutes every day doing chores.

a) How many days will it take for her to spend 378 minutes doing chores? ☐

3a 1 mark

b) How many minutes in March does Cacia spend doing chores? ☐

3b 1 mark

4 Yin Wai needs £28.95 to buy a new phone. She has £17.45 saved.

a) How much more money does Yin Wai need? ☐

4a 1 mark

b) If Yin Wai can earn £2.30 by walking the dog for her uncle, how many times would she need to walk the dog before she could buy the phone?

☐

4b 1 mark

Perimeter

Checking your understanding

1 Calculate the perimeter of these shapes.

a)

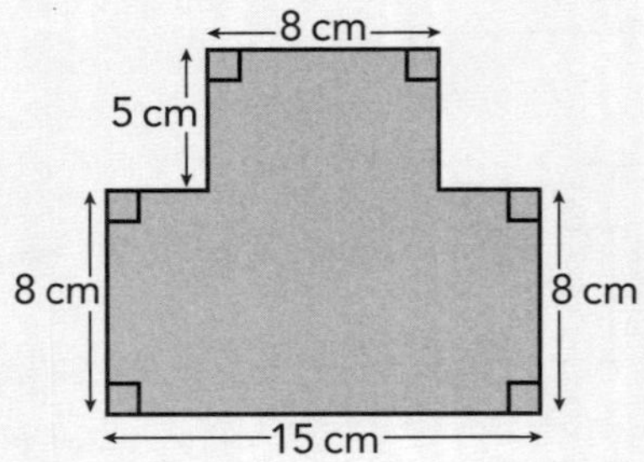

b)

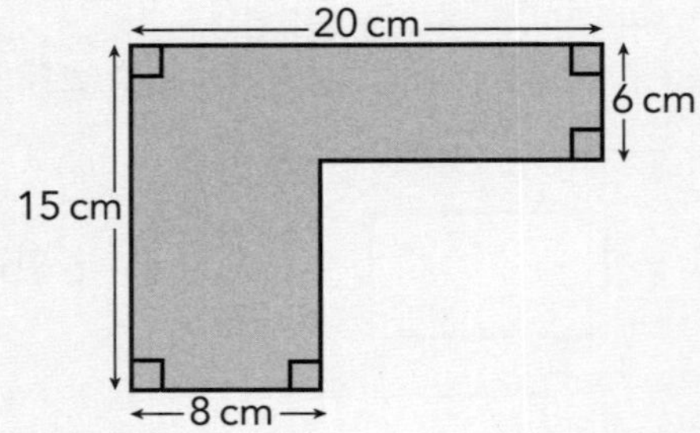

1a 2 marks

1b 2 marks

c)

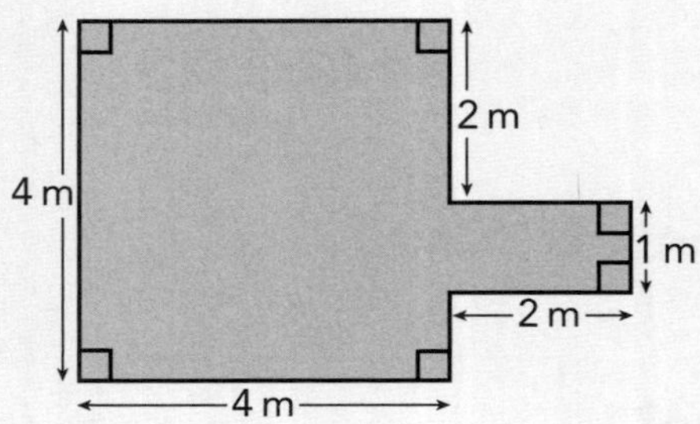

d)

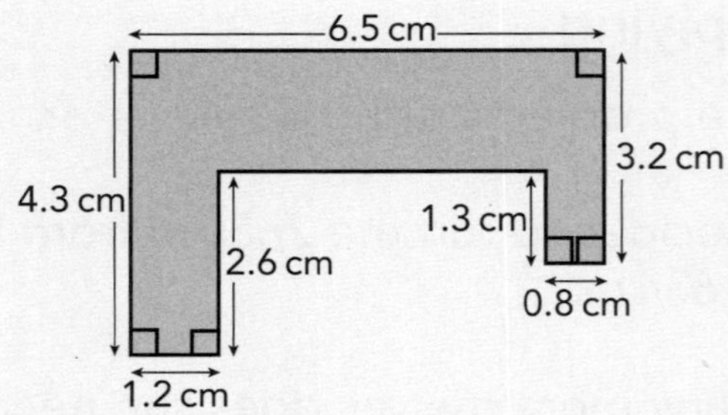

1c 2 marks

1d 2 marks

Using and applying

2

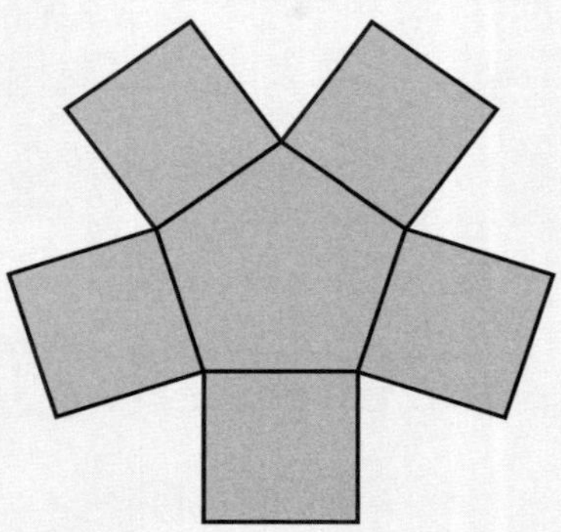

A regular pentagon has a side length of 8 cm. Morgan makes squares with the same side length and creates this design. What is the perimeter of the design?

2 2 marks

3

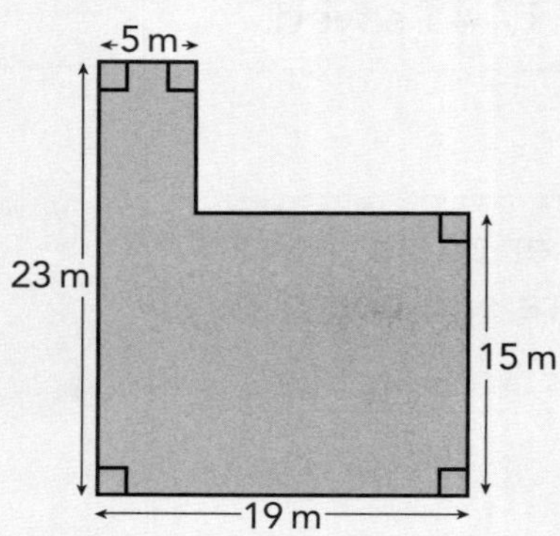

Mr Dupont puts a fence all round the perimeter of his yard. The fence costs £2 a metre. What is the cost of putting a fence all round the yard?

3 2 marks

The 24-hour clock

Checking your understanding

1 Write these times as they would appear on a 24-hour clock. 1 4 marks

a) 6:20 a.m. = ☐ **b)** 7:15 p.m. = ☐

c) 10 p.m. = ☐ **d)** 11:45 a.m. = ☐

2 Calculate how long it is between these two times:

a) 05:20 to 15:50 ☐ 2a 2 marks

b) 09:40 to 18:10 ☐ 2b 2 marks

c) 11:30 to 23:25 ☐ 2c 2 marks

d) 17:10 to 08:50 ☐ 2d 2 marks

Using and applying

3 Tegan hires a bike for 15 hours. If she hires it at 22:00, at what time will she have to return it? 3 2 marks

4 Cameron has a 24-hour alarm clock. He sleeps for 9 hours and 50 minutes. When he wakes up his alarm clock says 7:15. What time did the clock say when he went to sleep? 4 2 marks

5 Ali wants to fly to Australia. The flight takes 21 hours and 55 minutes. If the flight leaves at 15:40, at what time will it land? 5 2 marks

6 Hannah has friends over for her birthday. They spend the day together and then have a sleepover. They arrive at 11:30 a.m.

a) 11 hours and 50 minutes later, they go to bed. In 24-hour clock time, what time do they go to bed? 6a 2 marks

b) They leave at 8:50 a.m. the next day. How long were they with Hannah? 6b 2 marks

Reading scales

Checking your understanding

1 How much water is in each of these measuring cylinders?

a) ☐

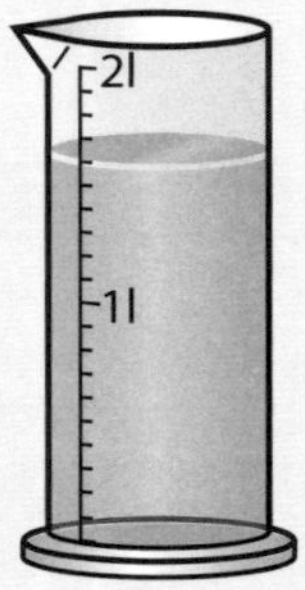

b) ☐

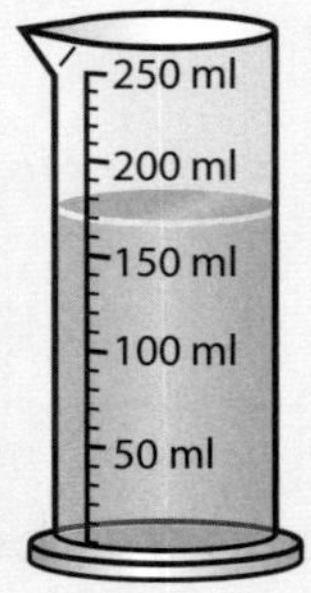

1a ☐ 1 mark

1b ☐ 1 mark

c) ☐

d) ☐

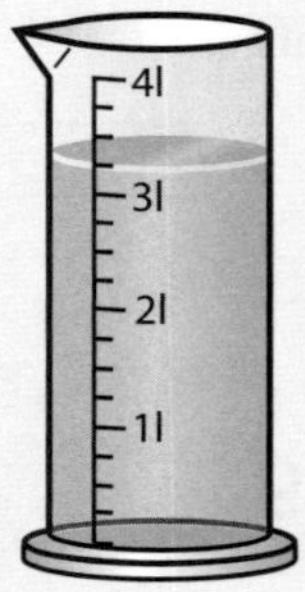

1c ☐ 1 mark

1d ☐ 1 mark

2 Mark 600 g on each of these scales.

a)

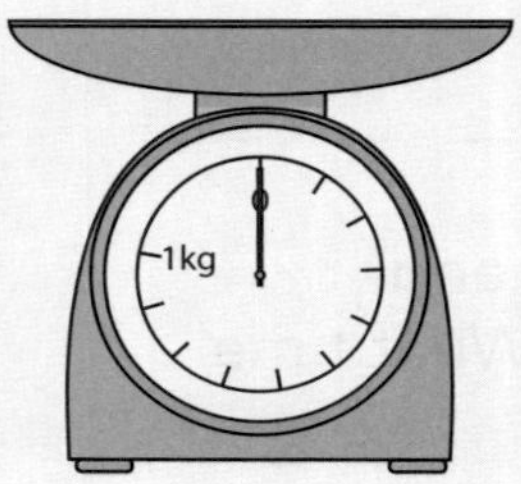

b)

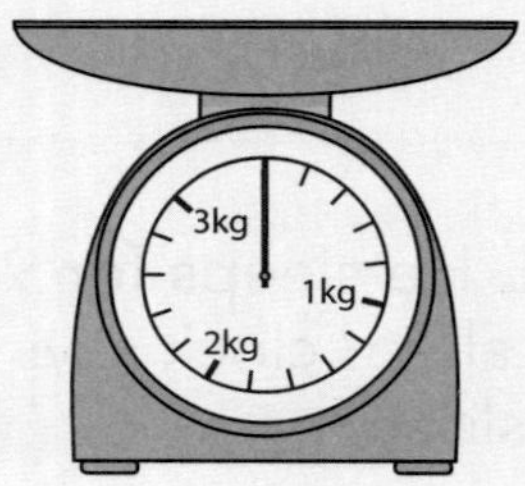

c)

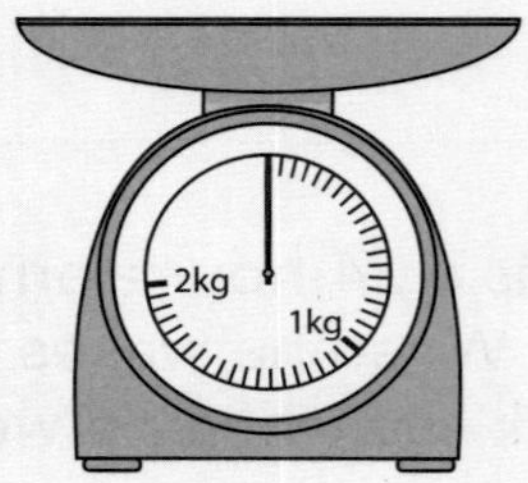

2 ☐ 3 marks

Using and applying

3

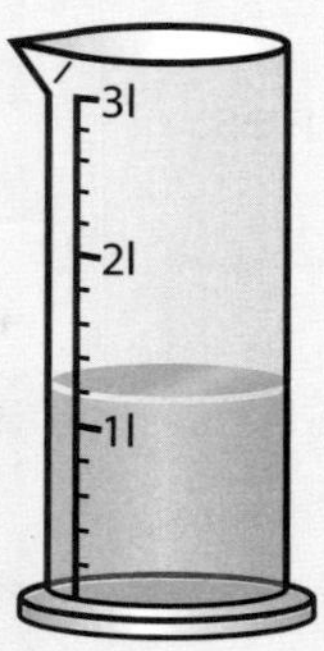

a) How much water is in the cylinder?

☐

3a ☐ 1 mark

b) Rachel pours in another 1500 ml of water. Mark the new water level on the measuring cylinder.

3b ☐ 1 mark

4

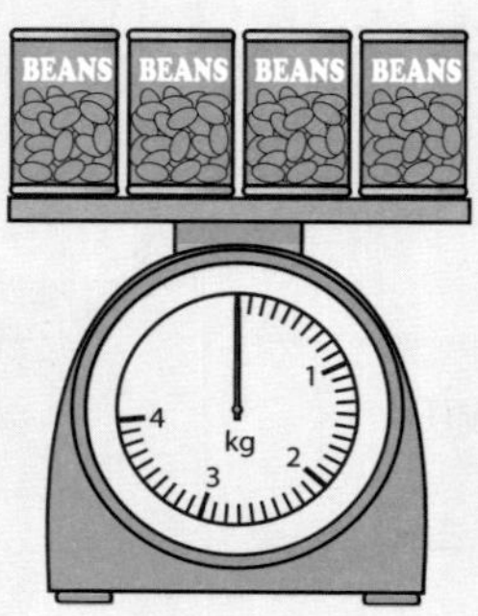

a) The 4 tins of beans weigh 2200 g altogether. Draw an arrow to show this on the scales.

4a ☐ 1 mark

b) One more tin is put on the scales. Mark with a star where the pointer will be with five tins on the scales.

4b ☐ 2 marks

Venn diagrams

Checking your understanding

1

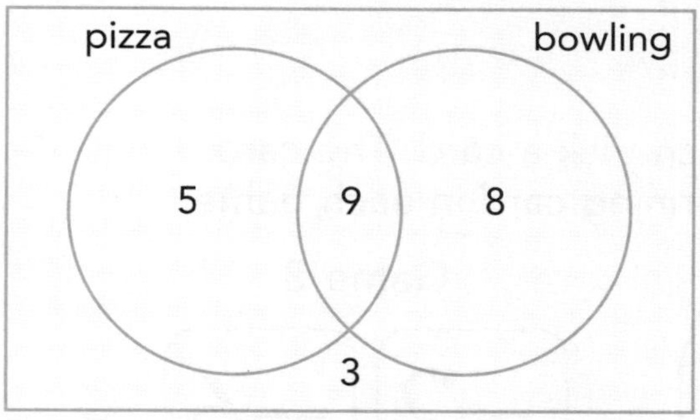

Some friends meet on a Saturday. Some go bowling, some go for a pizza.

a) How many friends went bowling? 1a 1 mark

b) How many ate pizza? 1b 1 mark

c) How many didn't go bowling or have a pizza? 1c 1 mark

d) How many friends went bowling and went for a pizza? 1d 1 mark

Using and applying

2

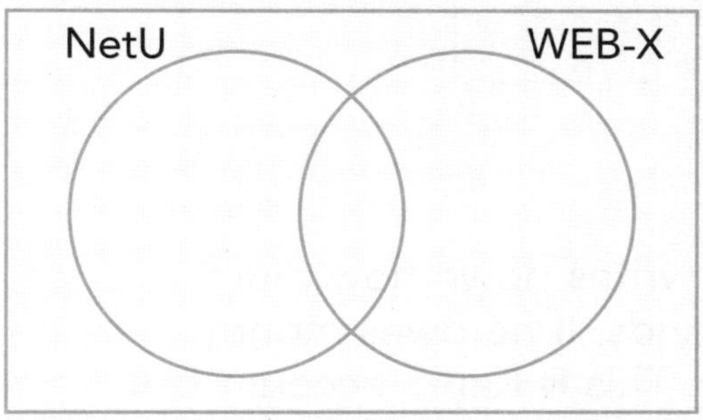

20 pupils attend the computer club. They all work on NetU or WEB-X. 5 pupils only use NetU. 12 pupils use both programs.

a) Fill in the information on the Venn diagram and fill in the empty parts of the Venn diagram. 2a 2 marks

b) How many pupils altogether used WEB-X? 2b 1 mark

3

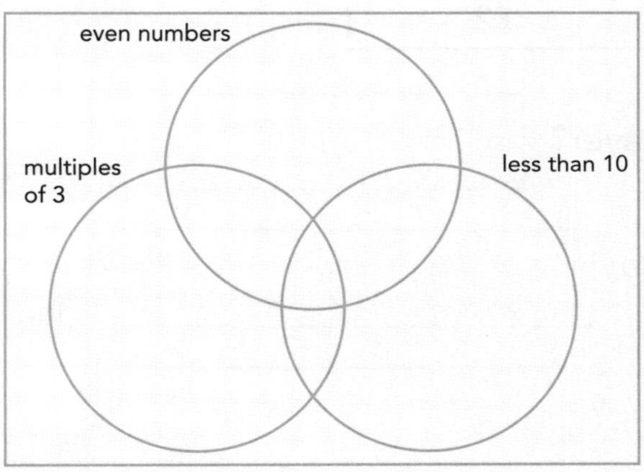

Put the numbers 1–15 in the correct place on this Venn diagram. 3 2 marks

Negative numbers

Checking your understanding

1 Rachel and Joe play a game where they each pick a card. The card with the highest number wins. Circle the winning card in each game.

Game 1		Game 2		Game 3	
1	−7	0	−4	−2	−6

1 — 3 marks

2 The temperature falls by 6°C at night. Write the night time temperature if these temperatures were the daytime temperatures:

a) 10°C ☐ **b)** 4°C ☐

c) 0°C ☐ **d)** −3°C ☐

2 — 4 marks

3 Put these temperatures in order, starting with the coldest.

6°C −7°C −3°C 0°C 2°C

☐ ☐ ☐ ☐ ☐

3 — 1 mark

Using and applying

4 Kani keeps an account of all his money. He writes down how much money he has and how much money he spends. If he owes money, he writes the amount as a negative number. This is Kani's account of his spending last month.

Date		My money
1st		£40
5th	Bought new MP3 player	−£15
11th	Sold PC Games	−£5
18th	Earned money by gardening	£2

a) How much did Kani pay for the MP3 player? ☐

4a — 1 mark

b) How much did he sell his PC games for? ☐

4b — 1 mark

c) How much money did he earn gardening? ☐

4c — 1 mark

5 Work out the value of the marked points on these number lines.

a) The difference between A and B on this number line is 40.
What are the values of A and B?

A = ☐ B = ☐

☐ 5a
2 marks

b) The difference between C and D on this number line is 75.
What are the values of C and D?

C = ☐ D = ☐

☐ 5b
2 marks

c) The difference between E and F on this number line is 33.
What are the values of E and F?

E = ☐ F = ☐

☐ 5c
2 marks

6 A rescue team reports its distance from sea level by measuring metres above sea level as positive numbers and metres below sea level as negative numbers.

a) A member of the rescue team dives to a depth of 10 m. What number would he use to report his distance from sea level?

☐ 6a
1 mark

b) A member of the team reports a distance of −4 m. He dives down another 8 m. What number will he report now?

☐ 6b
1 mark

c) One of the team reports a distance of −15 m and another member is on a hill 43 m above sea level. How far apart are the two team members?

☐ 6c
1 mark

d) A rescuer jumps from a helicopter 17 m above the sea. He falls a total distance of 25 m. What is the lowest point of his fall?

☐ 6d
1 mark

Reducing fractions

Checking your understanding

1 Write these fractions in their lowest terms.

a) $\frac{4}{8}$ = ☐ b) $\frac{5}{20}$ = ☐ c) $\frac{6}{15}$ = ☐

d) $\frac{8}{28}$ = ☐ e) $\frac{35}{50}$ = ☐ f) $\frac{48}{60}$ = ☐

g) $\frac{9}{36}$ = ☐ h) $\frac{50}{240}$ = ☐ i) $\frac{360}{480}$ = ☐

☐ 1
3 marks

2 Complete the fractions so they are equivalent:

a) $\frac{2}{7} = \frac{4}{\square} = \frac{\square}{35}$ b) $\frac{5}{6} = \frac{\square}{18} = \frac{45}{\square}$

☐ 2
2 marks

Using and applying

3 Jarmeen got 65 questions out of 100 questions correct in a test.
Write her mark as a fraction in its lowest form. ☐

☐ 3
1 mark

4 Three friends club together to buy a stunt kite. The kite costs £20.
Ben gave £4, James gave £5 and Lani gave £11.
Write the fraction of the total amount each person gave, making sure the fraction is in its lowest form.

Ben = ☐ James = ☐ Lani = ☐

☐ 4
3 marks

5 Joe did a test with 80 questions. How many questions did he get correct if he got the following fractions of the test right?

a) $\frac{1}{4} = \frac{\square}{80}$ questions correct

b) $\frac{5}{8} = \frac{\square}{80}$ questions correct

c) $\frac{17}{20} = \frac{\square}{80}$ questions correct

☐ 5a
1 mark

☐ 5b
1 mark

☐ 5c
1 mark

Total marks for this topic ☐

Ratio and proportion

Checking your understanding

1 Look at this pattern.

a) The ratio of white tiles to blue tiles is

1 mark 1a

b) The proportion of blue tiles is

1 mark 1b

2 **a)** Draw a line of 20 triangles and squares in the ratio 1:3.

1 mark 2a

b) What proportion of the shapes are squares?

1 mark 2b

3 ABBBBABBBBABBBBABBBB AAABAAABAAAB AABBBAABBBAABBBAABBB

a) Underline the pattern where the ratio of As to Bs is 1:4.

1 mark 3a

b) Circle the pattern where the proportion of Bs is $\frac{1}{4}$.

1 mark 3b

Using and applying

4 In Mr King's class, there are 2 girls for every 3 boys. If he has 30 children in his class, how many girls does he have?

2 marks 4

5 In a safari park, 2 in every 7 animals are monkeys. If there are 35 animals, how many monkeys are there?

2 marks 5

6 In her money box, Safi has silver and copper coins in the ratio 3:8. If she has 18 silver coins, how many coins does she have altogether?

2 marks 6

Total marks for this topic

Equivalent fractions, decimals and percentages

Checking your understanding

1 Write a fraction and a decimal that are equal to:

a) 40% fraction = ☐ decimal = ☐ 1a 1 mark

b) 70% fraction = ☐ decimal = ☐ 1b 1 mark

c) 64% fraction = ☐ decimal = ☐ 1c 1 mark

2 Match the equivalent amounts.

5% | 20% | 0.02 | 0.05

$\frac{1}{20}$ | 2% | $\frac{1}{5}$

2 5 marks

Using and applying

3 Which is larger, $\frac{3}{7}$ or $\frac{4}{9}$? Make sure you show your working!

3 2 marks

4 Which is larger, $\frac{5}{8}$ or 0.6? Make sure you show your working!

4 2 marks

5 Dayp eats $\frac{2}{5}$ of a pizza and Rachel eats 45%.

Who eats more?

Explain how you know.

5 2 marks

Total marks for this topic

Writing one number as a percentage of another

Checking your understanding

1 What percentage of 50 is 30? 1 mark

2 What percentage of 80 is 8? 1 mark

3 Express 15 as a percentage of 60. 1 mark

4 Express 10 as a percentage of 50. 1 mark

Using and applying

5 Rachel scores 18 out of 20 in a maths test.
What percentage did she get right? 1 mark

6 Cyla is practising shooting goals at netball.
She makes 40 attempts and scores 24 goals.
What is the percentage of shots that are successful? 1 mark

7 Sam spends 1 hour doing his homework.
He wastes 15 minutes drawing cartoons.
What percentage of his time does he use well? 1 mark

8 Winston's mum made 200 cakes for the school fair.
Winston ate 30 of them!
What percentage of the cakes did Winston eat? 1 mark

9 Yin Wai had written 500 words for her story.
She read 350 words.
What percentage of her story was this? 1 mark

10 Hannah cycled 5 km of a 25 km ride.
What percentage of the ride has she completed? 1 mark

Total marks for this topic

Checking your answers

Checking your understanding

1 Write an inverse operation sum for each of these calculations.

a) $342 + 275 = 617$ 1a 1 mark

b) $753 - 278 = 475$ 1b 1 mark

c) $73 \times 23 = 1679$ 1c 1 mark

d) $3233 \div 53 = 61$ 1d 1 mark

2 Write two different sums you could do to check these calculations.

a) $479 + 366 = 845$ 2a 2 marks

b) $4842 - 1765 = 3077$ 2b 2 marks

c) $46 \times 34 = 1564$ 2c 2 marks

d) $2856 \div 34 = 84$ 2d 2 marks

3 These sums will have an odd or even answer. Join them to the box that shows what type of answer they will have. Remember – you don't need to calculate the answers!

$3458 + 676$	odd	47×45
68×544		$5433 - 467$
$5688 - 3647$	even	$689 + 853$

3 3 marks

4 Use rounding to find an approximate answer for these sums.

a) $725 + 279 =$ ☐ $+$ ☐ $=$ ☐ 4a 2 marks

b) $742 - 311 =$ ☐ $-$ ☐ $=$ ☐ 4b 2 marks

c) $82 \times 22 =$ ☐ $\times$ ☐ $=$ ☐ 4c 2 marks

d) $824 \div 43 =$ ☐ $\div$ ☐ $=$ ☐ 4d 2 marks

Using and applying

5 $725 \times 23 = 3725$

Do you agree? YES NO

Explain why.

5 1 mark

6 $7425 - 2416 = 5012$

Do you agree? YES NO

Explain why.

6 1 mark

7 $5732 + 4759 = 9491$

Do you agree? YES NO

Explain why.

7 1 mark

Total marks for this topic

Decimal numbers and tables

Checking your understanding

1 Complete these sums.

a) 0.6 × 0.6 = ☐ b) 0.7 × 4 = ☐ c) 5 × 0.8 = ☐

1 ☐ 3 marks

2 Fill in the missing numbers.

a) 0.8 × 6 = ☐ b) 7 × ☐ = 2.1 c) 0.3 × ☐ = 0.09

d) ☐ × 0.5 = 3.5 e) 0.2 × 0.8 = ☐

2 ☐ 5 marks

Using and applying

3 Tegan saws a piece of wood into lengths of 0.4 m. If she cuts 8 lengths, how many metres of wood has she used?

3 ☐ 1 mark

4 Aadi runs 0.6 of a kilometre every day for a week. How many kilometres has he run altogether?

4 ☐ 1 mark

5 Dan uses 0.7 kg of flour every time he bakes for the school. He bakes 3 times over a period of ten days. How much flour does he use?

5 ☐ 1 mark

6 Fill in the missing numbers on this multiplication table.

×	3		0.9
0.2		0.4	
			0.63
	15		

6 ☐ 9 marks

Total marks for this topic ☐

Number properties

Checking your understanding

1 **a)** Prime numbers have [ ] factors. 1a 1 mark

b) The smallest prime number is [ ]. 1b 1 mark

2 **a)** Circle the common multiples of 3 and 4. 2a 1 mark

Multiples of 3 3 6 9 12 15 18 21 24 27 30

Multiples of 4 4 8 12 16 20 24 28 32

b) The lowest common multiple of 3 and 4 is [ ]. 2b 1 mark

3 Explain how to test if a number is divisible by 6. 3 2 marks

Using and applying

4 Which two prime numbers have a total of 8 and a difference of 2? 4 1 mark

5 Circle the numbers that are divisible by 3. 5 1 mark

548 381 5370 532 7833

6 Which of these numbers is divisible by both 4 and 9? [ ] 6 1 mark

672 549 252 748

7 Write the prime factors of 30. 7 1 mark

Total marks for this topic

Using brackets

Checking your understanding

1 Calculate:

a) $(3 + 5) \times 2 =$ 1a 1 mark

b) $3 + (5 \times 2) =$ 1b 1 mark

c) $(10 - 4) \div 2 =$ 1c 1 mark

d) $10 - (4 \div 2) =$ 1d 1 mark

e) $(36 + 12) \div 4 =$ 1e 1 mark

f) $36 + (12 \div 4) =$ 1f 1 mark

2 Complete these calculations.

a) $(123 + 489) - (24 \times 3) =$ 2a 1 mark

b) $(24 + 37) - (4 \times 5) =$ 2b 1 mark

c) $\frac{(175 - 90) \times (8 - 6)}{4 + (3 \times 2)} =$ 2c 1 mark

d) $\frac{(40 \times 4) \div (48 \div 3)}{(2.5 \times 4) \times 22} =$ 2d 1 mark

e) $\frac{(276 \div 12) + (500 - 388)}{5} =$ 2e 1 mark

f) $\frac{(35 \times 15) \div (42 + 9)}{7} =$ 2f 1 mark

Using and applying

3 Fill in the missing numbers.

a) $(7 + \square) \times 3 = 30$ — 3a, 1 mark

b) $(12 \div \square) \times 5 = 20$ — 3b, 1 mark

c) $80 \div (4 \times \square) = 4$ — 3c, 1 mark

d) $(43 + \square) \div 3 = 20$ — 3d, 1 mark

4 Use the problems to fill in and complete the bracket equations:

a) Sam bought a burger and milkshake for each of three friends. The burgers cost £1.72 and the milkshakes cost £1.10. What was the total cost?

$\square \times (\square + \square) = \square$ — 4a, 3 marks

b) Cyla read 30 pages every day for three weeks and then, on the next day, she read 45 pages. How many pages did she read altogether?

$(\square \times \square) + \square = \square$ — 4b, 3 marks

c) Mrs Cooper has 34 pupils. On Wednesday they all complete 30 questions in a maths quiz and 20 questions in a maths book. How many maths questions did Mrs Cooper have to mark on Wednesday?

$(\square) \times \square = \square$ — 4c, 3 marks

d) Mr Jackson buys each child in his class two sheets of stickers. One sheet has 15 stickers and the other has 12 stickers. If he has 24 children in his class, how many stickers does he buy altogether?

$(\square) \times \square = \square$ — 4d, 3 marks

Total marks for this topic $\square$

Adding and subtracting decimals

Checking your understanding

1 Write in the missing numbers.

a) 3.46 + 7.8 = ☐

b) 34.2 + ☐ = 75.13

c) 138.54 − ☐ = 75.7

d) 7.5 − 3.81 = ☐

e) 64.6 − ☐ = 28.82

f) ☐ + 27.3 = 583.2

g) 324.7 − 36.82 = ☐

h) 56.4 + 6.37 + 748.63 = ☐

1 — 8 marks

Using and applying

2 Callum collects 17.235 litres of water in a rain water butt. He uses 8.47 litres to water a vegetable patch. How much water is left in the water butt?

2 — 2 marks

3 Imogen collects 7.74 kg of litter. Cameron collects 9.955 kg. They sort the litter and put 13.644 kg of glass into the recycling bin. What weight of litter do they have left?

3 — 2 marks

4 Azim jumps 1.28 m and Sian jumps 1.82 m.

a) How much further does Sian jump than Azim?

4a — 2 marks

b) The school record is 1.95 m. How much further does Azim need to jump to match the record?

4b — 2 marks

5 46.2 thousand people log on to a website advertising the latest boy band. 18.65 thousand people buy their latest track. A further 8.58 thousand buy the full album. The rest log off without buying anything. How many thousands of people don't buy anything?

5 — 2 marks

Total marks for this topic

Multiplying and dividing decimals

Checking your understanding

1 Fill in the missing numbers.

a) $45.6 \times 100 =$ ☐

b) $576.1 \div$ ☐ $= 0.5761$

c) $1000 \times$ ☐ $= 56.49$

d) $86.356 \div 10 =$ ☐

1 — 4 marks

2 Calculate:

a) $8.43 \times 7.2 =$ ☐

b) $24.2 \times 9.8 =$ ☐

c) $56.4 \div 6 =$ ☐

d) $58.6 \div 0.4 =$ ☐

e) $75.3 \times (34.2 + 5.9) =$ ☐

f) $(29.4 - 8.72) \times 4.5 =$ ☐

2 — 6 marks

Using and applying

3 A bottle contains 1.4 litres of water. Caitlin shares the water equally between 4 jugs. How much water will there be in each jug?

3 — 2 marks

4 Every week Dan gets £5 pocket money. He always spends £1.59 on a magazine and a bar of chocolate. He saves the rest of his pocket money. How much will he save in 8 weeks?

4 — 2 marks

5 Harry lives 2.53 km away from school. If he has to walk to and from school for 3 days, how far will he have walked?

5 — 2 marks

6 A 10p coin has a diameter of 0.024 m. A line of 10p coins is made for charity. The line measures 15.792 m. How much money has been raised for charity?

6 — 2 marks

Total marks for this topic

Long multiplication

Checking your understanding

1 Calculate:

a) 35 × 286

b) 42 × 58

1 mark 1a

1 mark 1b

c) 653 × 34

d) 74 × 473

1 mark 1c

1 mark 1d

Using and applying

2 Callum does 26 press-ups every day for 3 weeks. How many press-ups does he do altogether?

2 marks 2

3 Talib puts 35p into his money box every day in July. How much money does he save?

2 marks 3

4 Whitney collects stamps. She sticks 44 stamps on each page in a book. The book has 125 pages. When she fills the book, how many stamps will she have altogether?

2 marks 4

Total marks for this topic

Long division

Checking your understanding

1 Calculate:

a) 945 ÷ 21

b) 1904 ÷ 56

c) 705 ÷ 15

d) 1392 ÷ 24

1a 1 mark

1b 1 mark

1c 1 mark

1d 1 mark

Using and applying

2 There are 1325 supporters going to watch Buxworth United play away. They hire 25 coaches and have exactly the right number of seats for everyone. How many seats must there be on each coach?

2 2 marks

3 A toy manufacturer makes 1984 toy cars. If the workers can pack 32 cars in box, how many boxes do they need for all the cars?

3 2 marks

4 A ticket to watch a hip-hop concert costs £18. If ticket sales make a total of £4770, how many tickets have been sold?

4 2 marks

Total marks for this topic

Fractions of amounts

Checking your understanding

1 a) $\frac{1}{3}$ of 36 = ☐ b) $\frac{2}{3}$ of 69 = ☐

c) $\frac{5}{11}$ of 66 = ☐ d) $\frac{9}{10}$ of 80 = ☐

e) $\frac{14}{15}$ of 60 = ☐ f) $\frac{7}{20}$ of 60 = ☐

1 — 6 marks

2 Fill in the missing numbers.

a) $\frac{1}{5}$ of ☐ = 20 b) $\frac{2}{3}$ of ☐ = 60

c) $\frac{3}{4}$ of ☐ = 45 d) $\frac{5}{8}$ of ☐ = 30

2 — 4 marks

Using and applying

3 Callum had to do 20 sums for homework. His brother did $\frac{1}{4}$ of them, his Nan did $\frac{3}{10}$, his mum did $\frac{7}{20}$ and Callum did the rest. How many sums did Callum do?

3 — 2 marks

4 40 people wanted to download music. The computer system crashed and only $\frac{3}{8}$ of them managed to complete the download. How many people could **not** download the music they wanted?

4 — 2 marks

5 60 children signed up for baseball coaching. The club could only take $\frac{3}{5}$ of them. How many children could attend the coaching session?

5 — 2 marks

Total marks for this topic

ACHIEVE LEVEL 5

MATHEMATICS

Answers for Practice Questions

RISING STARS

Page 8

1 a) 17, 20 b) 37, 43 c) 9.0, 10.2
d) 113, 164 e) 2, −4 f) 201, 220

2 a) 16 b) 8th

3 No. The difference between the numbers is 3, 4 so will continue 5, 6, 7, and so on. The next two terms should be 18, 24.

4 a) £1.40
b) £4.50 *(2 marks; allow 1 mark for incorrect answer but evidence of correct working)*

Page 9

1 a) 1316 b) 308 c) 214.5
d) 2385 e) 2.508 f) 430
g) 85.99 h) −61.47

2 a) 1016 b) 5300

3 a) 14 b) 837 minutes

4 a) £11.50 (NOT £11.5) b) 5

Page 10

1 *(**1a** to **1d**: 2 marks each; allow 1 mark for incorrect answer but evidence of correct working)*
a) 56 cm b) 70 cm
c) 20 m d) 24.4 cm

2 120 cm *(2 marks; allow 1 mark for incorrect answer but evidence of correct working)*

3 £168 *(2 marks; allow 1 mark for incorrect answer but evidence of correct working)*

Page 11

1 a) 06:20 b) 19:15
c) 22:00 d) 11:45

2 *(**2a** to **2d**: 2 marks each; allow 1 mark for incorrect answer but evidence of correct working)*
a) 10 hours 30 minutes
b) 8 hours and 30 minutes
c) 11 hours and 55 minutes
d) 15 hours and 40 minutes

(3 to 6b: 2 marks each; allow 1 mark for incorrect answer but evidence of correct working)

3 13:00 hours

4 21:25

5 13:35

6 a) 23:20 b) 21 hours and 20 minutes

Page 12

1 a) 1600 ml or 1.6 litres b) 170 ml
c) 2400 ml or 2.4 litres
d) 3250 ml or 3.25 litres

2 Mark 600 g on each of these scales.

a) 

b) 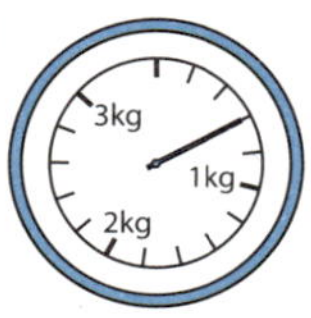

c) 

3 a) 1200 ml or 1.2 litres
b) 

4 a) 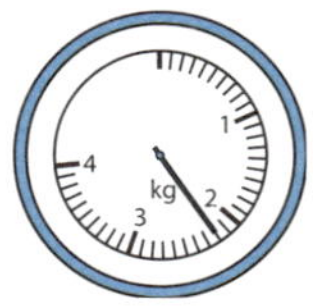

b) 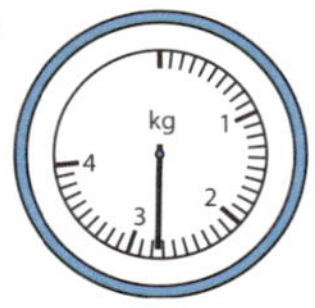

(2 marks)

Page 13

1 a) 17 b) 14 c) 3 d) 9

2 a) 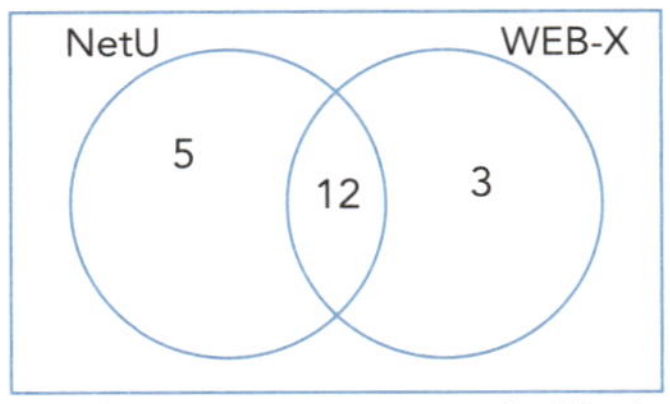

(1 mark for 2 sections correctly filled in, 2 marks for all correct)

b) 15

3 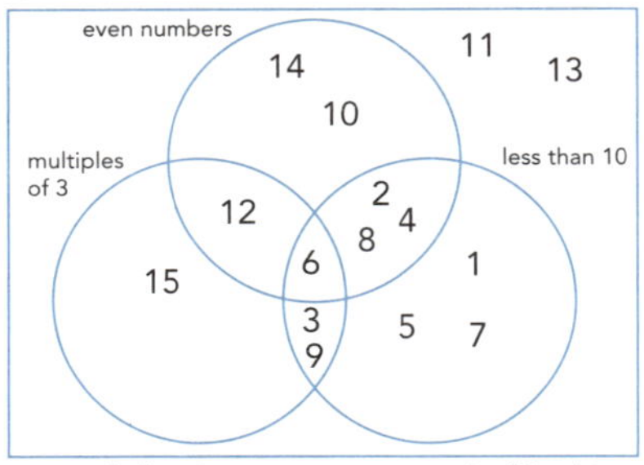

(1 mark for 4 sections correctly filled in, 2 marks for all correct)

Pages 14–15

1 Game 1 = 1, Game 2 = 0, Game 3 = −2

2 a) 4°C b) −2°C c) −6°C d) −9°C

3 −7°, −3°C, 0°C, 2°C, 6°C

4 a) £55 b) £10 c) £7

5 A = −24 B = 16 C = −30
D = 45 E = −44 F = −11

6 a) −10 m b) −12 m
c) 58 m d) −8 m

Page 16

1 a) $\frac{1}{2}$ b) $\frac{1}{4}$ c) $\frac{2}{5}$ d) $\frac{2}{7}$ e) $\frac{7}{10}$
f) $\frac{4}{5}$ g) $\frac{1}{4}$ h) $\frac{5}{24}$ i) $\frac{3}{4}$
(1 mark for each 3 correct)

2 a) $\frac{4}{14}$, $\frac{10}{35}$ *(1 mark for **both** fractions correct)*
b) $\frac{15}{18}$, $\frac{45}{54}$ *(1 mark for **both** fractions correct)*

3 $\frac{13}{20}$

4 Ben $\frac{1}{5}$ James $\frac{1}{4}$ Lani $\frac{11}{20}$

5 a) 20 b) 50 c) 68

Page 17

1 a) 2:5 b) $\frac{5}{7}$

2 a) △ □□△ □□△ □□△ □□△ □□
b) $\frac{3}{4}$

3 a) ABBB pattern underlined
b) AAAB pattern circled

(4 to 6: 2 marks each; allow 1 mark for evidence of correct working but incorrect answer)

4 12

5 10

6 66

Page 18

1 a) $\frac{2}{5}$ (or equivalent), 0.4
b) $\frac{7}{10}$ (or equivalent), 0.7
c) $\frac{16}{25}$ (or equivalent), 0.64 *(1 mark for each 2 correct)*

2 *(1 mark for each line correct, deduct 1 mark for each incorrect line)*

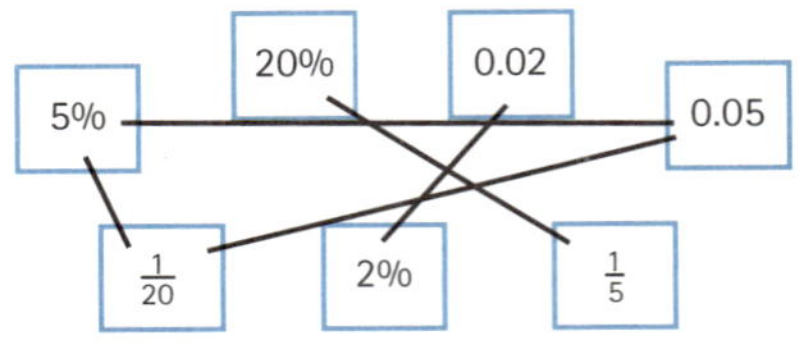

(3 to 5: 2 marks each for correct working and answer; 1 mark for correct method of working but incorrect answer)

3 $\frac{3}{7} = \frac{27}{63}$ and $\frac{4}{9} = \frac{28}{63}$ so $\frac{4}{9}$ is larger

4 e.g. $\frac{5}{8}$ = 0.625, which is larger than 0.6

5 e.g. $\frac{2}{5}$ = 0.4 = 40% which is less than 45%, so Rachel eats more

Page 19

1 60% 2 10%

3 25% 4 20%

5 90% 6 60%

7 75% 8 15%

9 70% 10 20%

Pages 20–21

1 a) 617 − 275 = 342 or 617 − 342 = 275
b) 475 + 278 = 753
c) 1679 ÷ 23 = 73 or 1679 ÷ 73 = 23
d) 53 × 61 = 3233

2 a) 366 + 479 = 845, 845 − 366 = 479, 845 − 479 = 366 *(1 mark each sum; max 2 marks)*
b) 3077 + 1765 = 4842, 4842 − 3077 = 1765 *(1 mark each sum)*
c) 34 × 46 = 1564, 1564 ÷ 34 = 46, 1564 ÷ 46 = 34 *(1 mark each sum; max 2 marks)*
d) 34 × 84 = 2856, 2856 ÷ 84 = 34 *(1 mark each sum)*

3 *(1 mark for each 2 lines correct)*

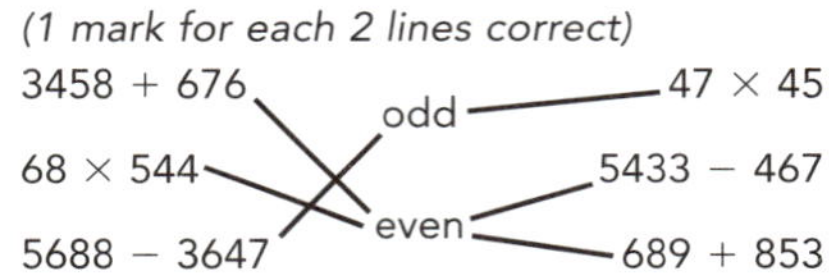

4 *(4a to 4d: 2 marks each)*
a) 700 + 300 = 1000
b) 700 − 300 = 400
c) 80 × 20 = 1600
d) 800 ÷ 40 = 20

5 No. 700 × 20 = 14,000 which is not near to 3725.

6 No. Odd – even should have an odd answer.

7 No. 5000 + 4000 = 9000 but 700 + 700 would be more than another 1000.

Page 22

1 a) 0.36 b) 2.8 c) 4 or 4.0

2 a) 4.8 b) 0.3 c) 0.3
d) 7 e) 0.16

3 3.2 m

4 4.2 km

5 2.1 kg

6 *(1 mark for each number correct)*

×	3	2	0.9
0.2	0.6	0.4	0.18
0.7	2.1	1.4	0.63
5	15	10	4.5

Page 23

1 a) 2 b) 2
2 a) 12 and 24 **both** circled b) 12
3 Check if it is even *(1 mark)* and add the digits to see if the sum of the digits is divisible by 3 *(1 mark)*
4 3 and 5
5 381, 5370, 7833 *(**all** circled for 1 mark)*
6 252
7 2, 3 and 5 *(**all** for one mark)*

Pages 24–25

1 a) 16 b) 13 c) 3
d) 8 e) 12 f) 39
2 a) 540 b) 41 c) 17
d) $\frac{1}{22}$ e) 27 f) 1.47
3 a) 3 b) 3 c) 5 d) 17
*(**4a** to **4d**: 1 mark for equation completed correctly, further 2 marks for correct answer; allow 1 mark for correct working but incorrect answer)*
4 a) 3 × (£1.72 + £1.10) = £8.46
b) (30 × 21) + 45 = 675
c) (30 + 20) × 34 = 1700
d) (15 + 12) × 24 = 648

Page 26

1 a) 11.26 b) 40.93 c) 62.84
d) 3.69 e) 35.78 f) 555.9
g) 287.88 h) 811.4
*(**2** to **5**: 2 marks for each question; allow 1 mark for correct method but incorrect answer)*
2 8.765 litres
3 4.051 kg
4 a) 0.54 m b) 0.67 m
5 18.97

Page 27

1 a) 4560 b) 1000
c) 0.05649 d) 8.6356
2 a) 60.696 b) 237.16 c) 9.4
d) 146.5 e) 3019.53 f) 93.06
3 0.35 litres
4 £27.28
5 15.18 km
6 £65.80

Page 28

1 a) 10,010 b) 2436
c) 22,202 d) 35,002
*(**2** to **4**: 2 marks each for correct answer; 1 mark for evidence of correct working but incorrect answer)*
2 546
3 1085p or £10.85
4 5500

Page 29

1 a) 45 b) 34 c) 47 d) 58
*(**2** to **4**: 2 marks each for correct answer; 1 mark for evidence of correct working but incorrect answer)*
2 53
3 62
4 265

Page 30

1 a) 12 b) 46 c) 30 d) 72
e) 56 f) 21
2 a) 100 b) 90 c) 60 d) 48
*(**3** to **5**: 2 marks for each question; 1 mark for evidence of correct working but incorrect answer)*
3 2
4 25
5 36

Page 31

1 a) 8 b) 48 c) 6 d) 56
2 a) 200 b) 300
3 33 *(2 marks for correct answer; 1 mark for evidence of correct working but incorrect answer)*
4 56 *(2 marks for correct answer; 1 mark for evidence of correct working but incorrect answer)*

Pages 32–33

1 a) A (3, 5), B (−1, 6), C (−4, −3), D (2, −2)
b)

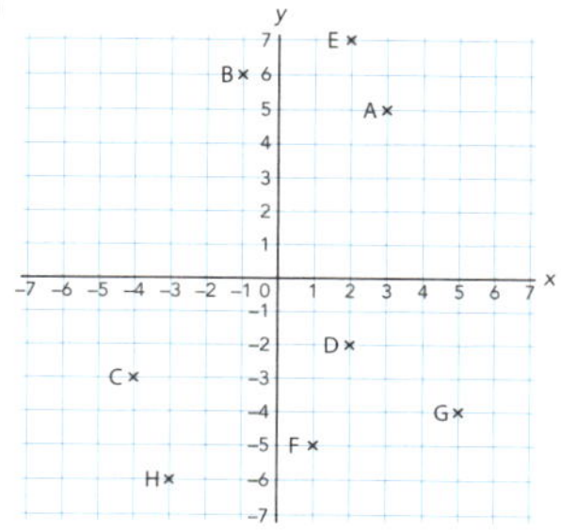

2 a) (−3, −1) b) (2, 0)
3 a) in either order: (−3, −5) and (5, 3) *(2 marks)*
b) (1, −1), (3, 1), (−1, −3), (5, 3) *(2 marks for all correct, 1 mark for 2 or more correct)*
c) The second number is 2 less than the first in each pair of coordinates.
d) (10, 8), (−6, −8) *(2 marks)*
4 (8, 10) *(1 mark for each coordinate)*

Page 34

a)

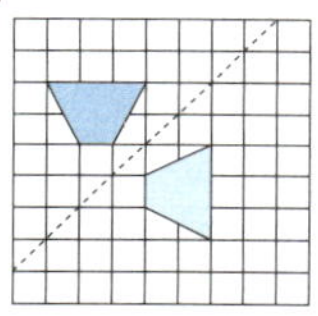

order of rotational symmetry = 1

b)

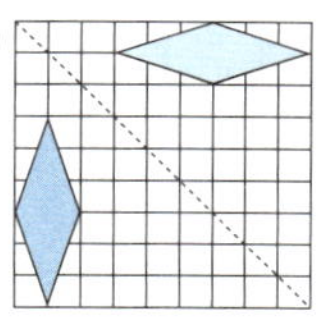

order of rotational symmetry = 2

c)

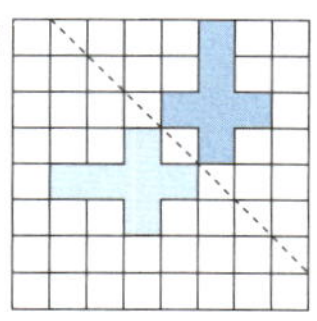

order of rotational symmetry = 4

d)

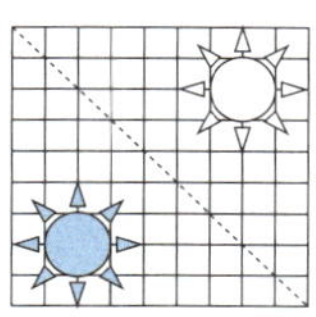

order of rotational symmetry = 8

Page 35

1 *(allow 1 mark for correct horizontal move and 1 for correct vertical move; 4 marks total)*
a)

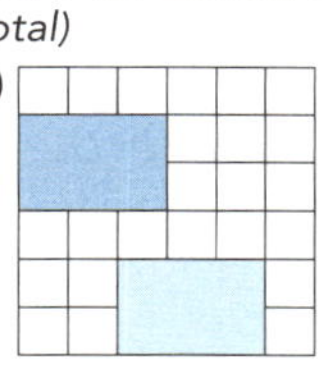

b)

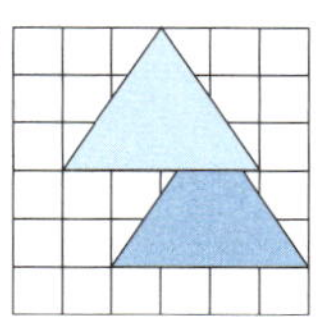

2 a) C b) B
c) (−7, −1) **or** 7 left and 1 down
d) (10, −2) **or** 10 right and 2 down
e) (10, 2) **or** 10 right and 2 up

Page 36

1 a)

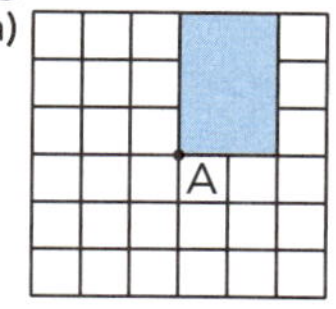

b)

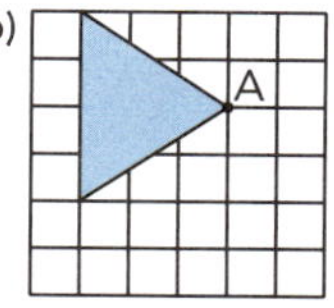

2 a)

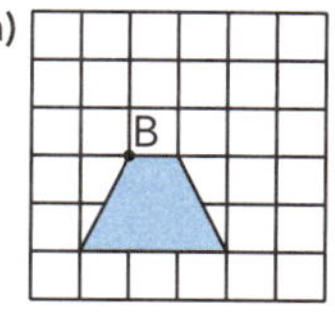

b)

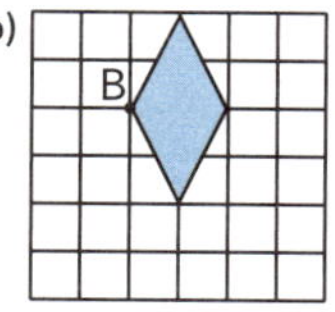

3 a)

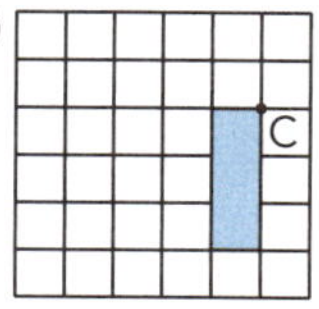

b)

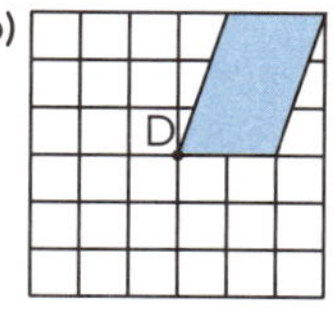

4 a)

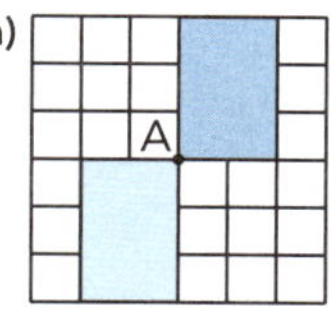

b)

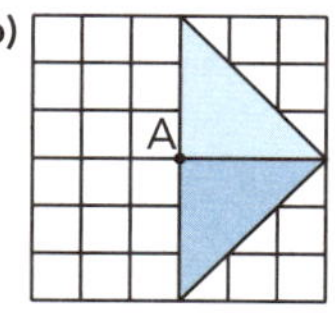

a) clockwise **or** anticlockwise 180°
b) anticlockwise 90° **or** clockwise 270°

Page 37

1 Check angles by measuring *(2 marks for accurate; 1 mark for ± 2°)*
2 a) 25° b) 78° c) 147° d) 170°
3 a) 85° b) 34 mm

Page 38

1 a) 27° b) 63° c) 45° d) 52°
2 a) 59° b) 29° c) 67° d) 129°
3 25°

Page 39

1 55° *(2 marks)*
2 11
3 18°
4 a) 237° b) 213° c) 33°

Pages 40–41

1 a) ÷ 10 b) ÷ 1000 c) × 1000
d) ÷ 10
2 a) answer in range 2–3 cm b) 3
c) 2–2.2 lbs d) 30 cm
e) 25 g f) 1.75–2 pints
3 a) 0.325 b) 4.325 c) 0.21
d) 3 e) 400 f) 13
4 a) decilitres b) mm c) m
d) ml e) cg f) dm
5 a) 14 b) 56 m
6 10 *(2 marks; allow 1 mark for incorrect answer with evidence of correct working)*
7 6 kg is about 12 lb for £2.40; 6 lb costs £1.40 so 12 lb would cost £2.80. So 6 kg for £2.40 is better value. *(2 marks; allow 1 mark for incorrect answer with evidence of correct working)*
8 64
9 a) green *(1 mark)*
Blue = 7.8 m, red = 0.9 m, green = 8 m, so there is most green *(1 mark)*
b) 16.7 m or 1670 cm or 16,700 mm *(2 marks; allow 1 mark for incorrect answer with evidence of correct working)*

Pages 42–43

*(**1a** to **6**, allow 2 marks; 1 mark for evidence of correct working but incorrect answer)*

1 **a)** 96 cm^2 **b)** 120 cm^2
 c) 290 cm^2 **d)** 192 m^2
2 **a)** 70 m^2 **b)** 54 cm^2
3 5 cm
4 54 m^2
5 £396
6 120 m^2

Page 44

1 **a)** mean = 4, median = 5
 b) mean = 3, median = 2
 c) mean = 5, median = 4.5 *(6 marks total)*
2 mean = 5.8, median = 5.9, mode = 3.6, range = 6
3 mean = 62, median = 82, mode = 82, range = 88

Page 45

1 **a)** Data set A: mode = 0 median = 1
 range = 15 mean = 6
 Data set B: mode = 7 median = 4
 range = 10 mean = 5
 b) A; B
2 Stilts mean = 20; median = 18
 Space hoppers mean = 21; median = 22
 Since both the mean and median are higher for the space hoppers, they are the more popular pieces of equipment.
 (6 marks; 1 mark for each mean and median correctly calculated, 2 marks for the explanation)
3 TopX mode is 10, range = 4
 King mode = 9, range = 4
 Since the ranges are equal, and the mode for TopX is higher than for the King, TopX appears to have a higher average age than the King group.
 (6 marks; 1 mark for each mode and range correctly calculated, 2 marks for the explanation)

Page 46

a i) answers around €1.3
 ii) answers around €6.50
 iii) £20 = €26
b) answers around €58.50
(for questions c to e: 2 marks each; 1 mark for evidence of correct working but incorrect answer)
c) No. £24 is about €30 and he sold it for €28 so he lost €2
d) answers around £10
e) answers around €4

Page 47

1 **a)**

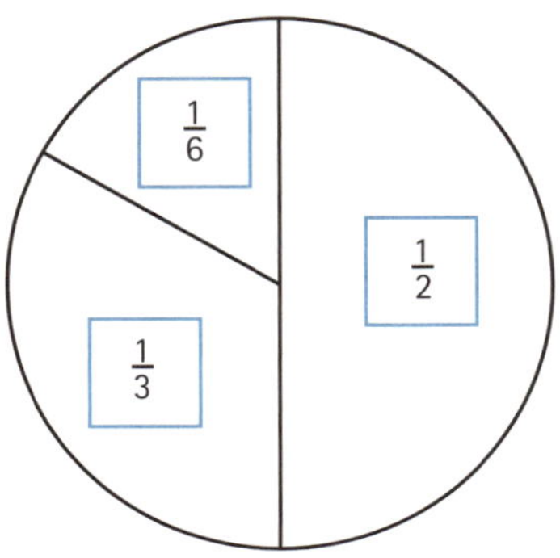

b)

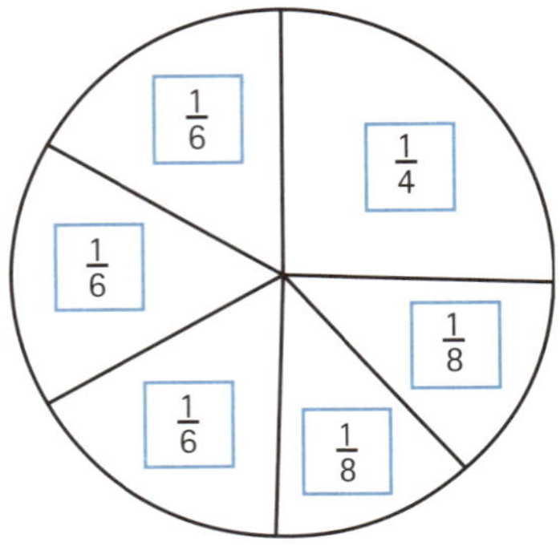

(1 mark per type of fraction correct)
 b) any $\frac{1}{8}$ fraction coloured
2 **a)** 5 **b)** one of $\frac{1}{11}$; $\frac{1}{12}$; $\frac{1}{13}$
 c) 50% **d)** 8–12%
 e) Hannah's class. $\frac{1}{3}$ of the children in Hannah's class watch for 1–2 hours = 12 children; $\frac{1}{2}$ of the children in Sam's class watch for 1–2 hours = 10 children, so more children in Hannah's class watch 1–2 hours TV.

Pages 48–49

1 *(2 marks; 1 mark for 3 or more correct)*
 A I will grow an extra leg tonight.
 B One day, I will go to the moon.
 C When I throw a die I will get a 5 or a 6.
 D If I toss a coin, I will get a head.
 E It will snow in January.
 F It will get dark tonight.
2 No, the probability of getting a head or a tail is always $\frac{1}{2}$.
3 **a)** $\frac{1}{6}$ **b)** $\frac{1}{6}$
 c) $\frac{1}{2}$ (or equivalent) **d)** 0
4 **a)** $\frac{3}{10}$ **b)** $\frac{1}{2}$ (or equivalent)
 c) $\frac{3}{5}$ (or equivalent) **d)** 0
5 **a)** 10 **b)** $\frac{1}{4}$ (or equivalent) **c)** 2
 d)

Apple juice	3	2	1	0
Orange juice	0	1	2	3

 (2 marks)
6 $\frac{3}{8}$

Pages 50–51

1 **a)** 2 **b)** 6 **c)** 5 **d)** 52
2 A = (N ÷ 8) − 4
3 A = (N + 3) × 6 or A = 6 (N + 3)
4 **a)** H = T ÷ P or H = $\frac{T}{P}$
 b) H = T ÷ 5
5 **a)** T = (P × E) + C **b)** £225
6 **a)** D = ST or D = S × T
 b) D = 3.6 × 8 = 28.8 m
 c) 22 = S × 4
7 A = 40, B = 20, C = 20 *(2 marks; 1 mark for evidence of correct working but incorrect answer)*
8 D = 30, E = 10 *(2 marks; 1 mark for evidence of correct working but incorrect answer)*

Pages 52–53

*(**1** to **4**: 2 marks each; 1 mark for evidence of correct working but incorrect answer)*
1 25
2 3, 3, 5, 9, 10
3

21	6
4	4

4 £45.30
5 **a)** 4001–4100 m **b)** 17:45
 c) 2 hours and 15 mins *(2 marks; 1 mark for evidence of correct working but incorrect answer)*
6 £1200 *(2 marks; 1 mark for evidence of correct working but incorrect answer)*

Pages 54–55

*(**1** to **8**: 2 marks; 1 mark for evidence of correct working but incorrect answer)*
1 8
2 32
3 $3\frac{3}{4}$ hours
4 64%
5 45
6 16
7 **a)** £175 **b)** £170
8 6

Pages 56–57

1 3.5 m *(2 marks; 1 mark for evidence of correct working but incorrect answer)*
2 3 eggs, 75 g butter, 1200 ml milk, 150 g rice, 120 g sugar *(5 marks)*
3 1800 ml or 1.8 litres *(2 marks; 1 mark for evidence of correct working but incorrect answer)*
4 Cameron = 8 stone, Imogen = 4 stone, Dad = 12 stone *(2 marks; 1 mark for evidence of correct working but incorrect answer)*
5 **a)** 08:35
*(**5b** to **d**): 2 marks each; 1 mark for evidence of correct working but incorrect answer)*
 b) 42 minutes
 c) $\frac{23}{53}$
 d) 1 hour 10 minutes, or 70 minutes

Pages 58–59

1 **a)** 64 cm **b)** 96 cm^2 *(2 marks; 1 mark for evidence of correct working but incorrect answer)*
2 kite
*(**3a** to **4b**: 2 marks for each question; 1 mark for evidence of correct working but incorrect answer)*
3 **a)** 96 cm **b)** 432 cm^2
4 **a)** 120° **b)** 60°
5 **a)** Both are correct.
 b) It can be reflected in the mirror line as shown or it could be translated (3, −3).

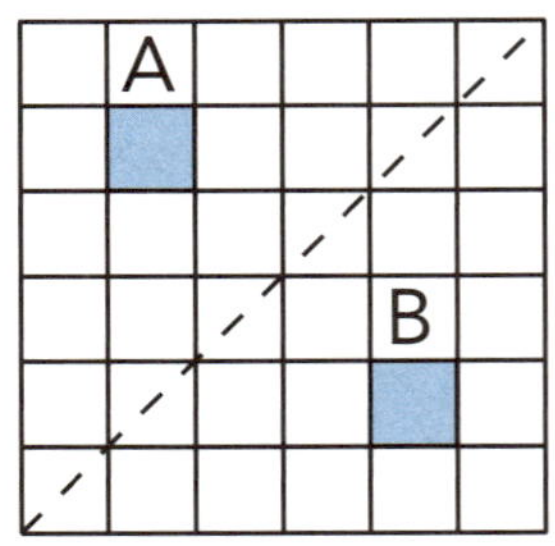

(2 marks)

*(**6** to **8b**: 2 marks for each question; 1 mark for evidence of correct working but incorrect answer)*
6 18 cm^2
*(**7a** to **8b**: 2 marks for each question; 1 mark for evidence of correct working but incorrect answer)*
7 **a)** 60 cm **b)** 1800 cm^2
8 **a)** 150 cm^2 **b)** 125 cm^3

Calculating percentages of amounts

Checking your understanding

1 Calculate:

a) 40% of 20

b) 60% of 80

1 mark 1a

1 mark 1b

c) 15% of 40

d) 35% of 160

1 mark 1c

1 mark 1d

2 Fill in the missing numbers.

a) 40% of ☐ = 80

b) 20% of ☐ = 60

2 marks 2

Using and applying

3 60 children went on a school visit to Stratford. 45% of them had been there before. How many had **not** visited Stratford before?

2 marks 3

4 Yani started a penny collection to pay for the adoption of a child in Indonesia. Of the 280 pennies given on the first morning, Yani gave 20%. How many pennies did he give?

2 marks 4

Total marks for this topic

Coordinates

Checking your understanding

1

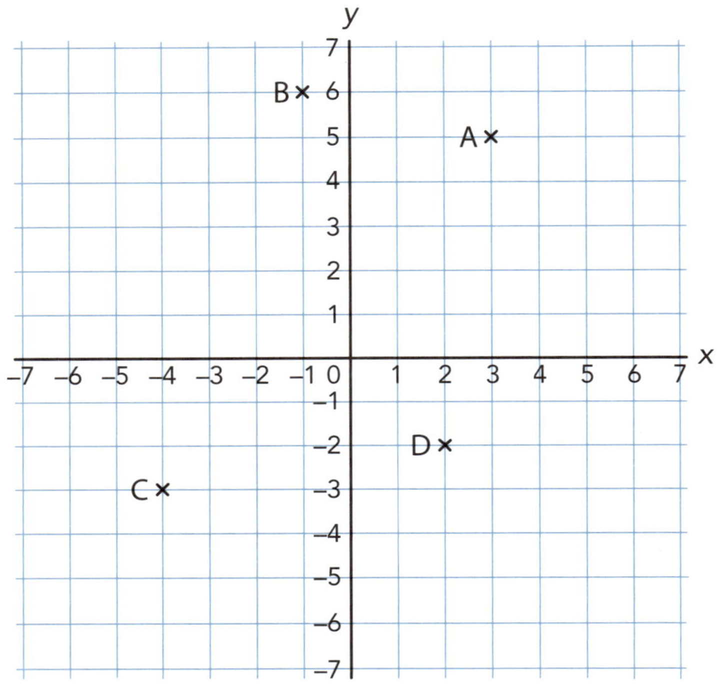

a) Write the coordinates of the points.

A

B

C

D

1a
4 marks

b) Mark these points on the grid.
E (2, 7)   F (1, −5)   G (5, −4)   H (−3, −6)

1b
4 marks

Using and applying

2

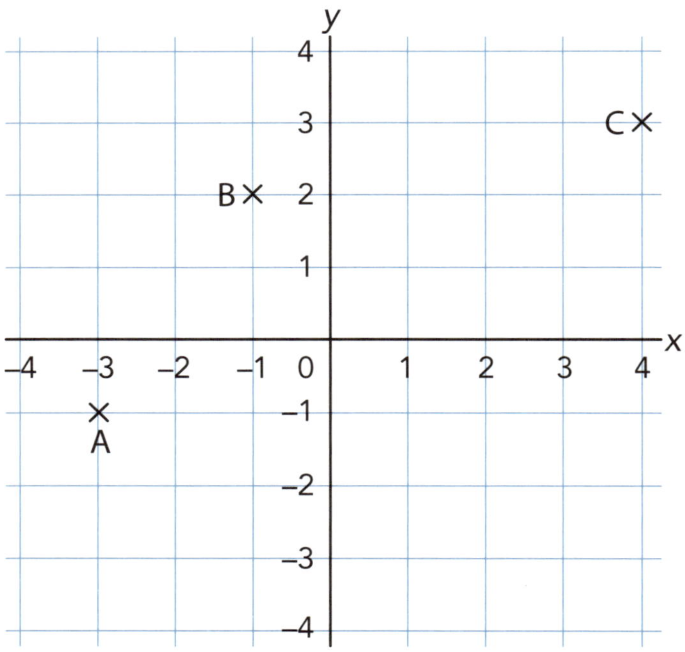

a) What are the coordinates of A?

2a
1 mark

b) Write the coordinates of point D so that ABCD makes a parallelogram.

2b
1 mark

3

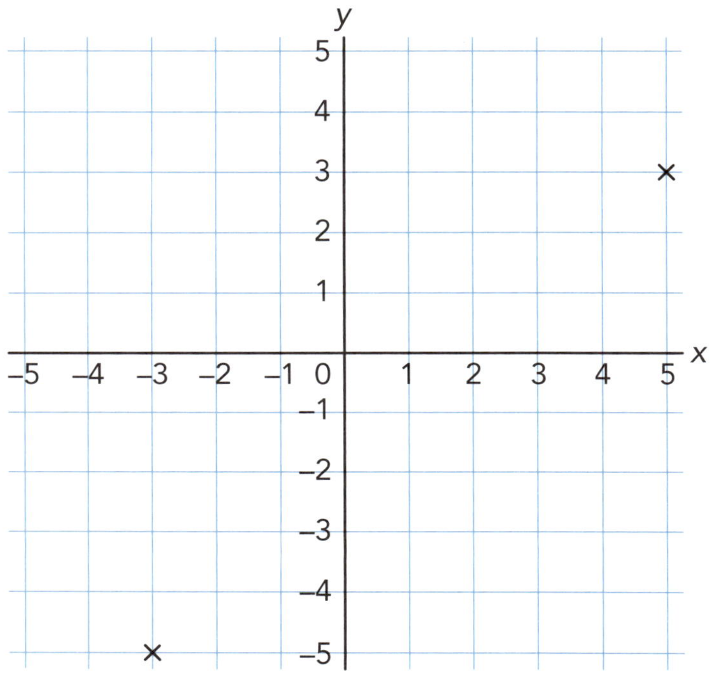

A long, straight line can be drawn that passes through the crosses on this grid.

a) What are the coordinates of the crosses?

3a 2 marks

b) Circle the coordinates through which the line would pass.

(1, −1) (3, 1) (2, −2) (2, 4) (−1, −3) (5, 3) (−2, 0)

3b 2 marks

c) Look at the coordinates you have circled. Describe any patterns you see.

3c 1 mark

d) If the grid was made bigger and the line extended, complete these coordinates that the line would pass through.

A (10,) B (, −8)

3d 2 marks

4 A rectangle ABCD is drawn on a pair of axes.

What are the coordinates of point B?

4 2 marks

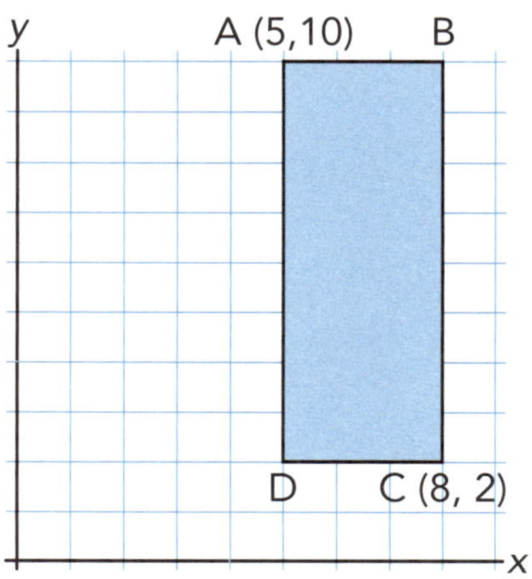

Total marks for this topic

Symmetries of 2-D shapes

Checking your understanding

Reflect each shape in the mirror line. Write the order of rotational symmetry for each shape.

a) order of rotational symmetry = ☐

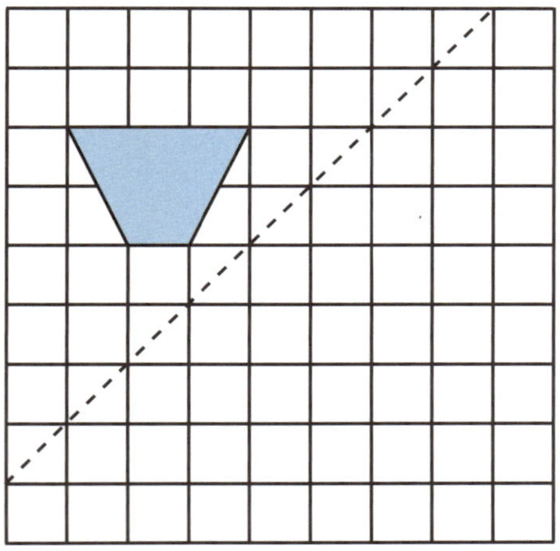

b) order of rotational symmetry = ☐

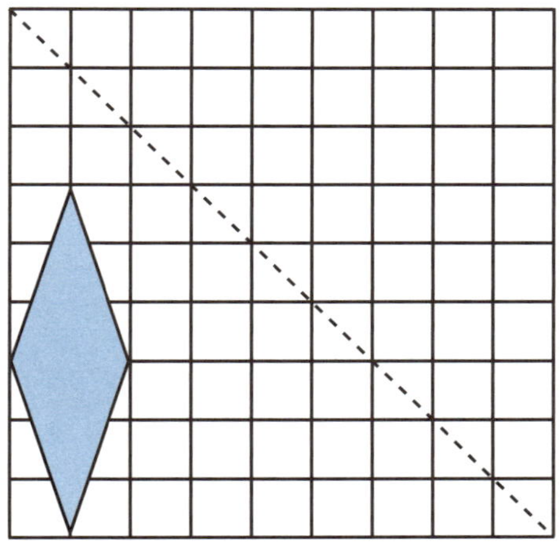

c) order of rotational symmetry = ☐

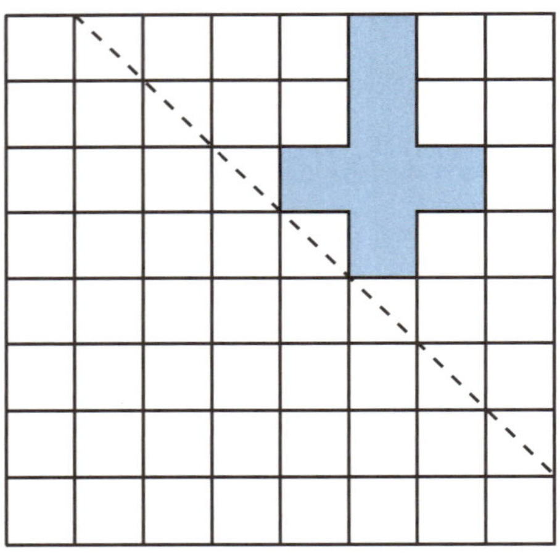

d) order of rotational symmetry = ☐

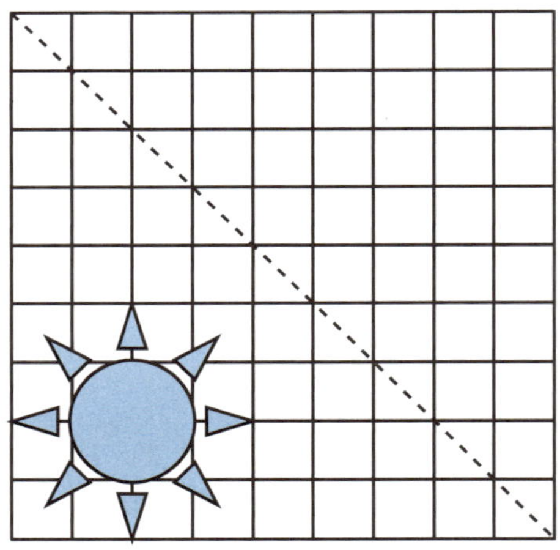

a 3 marks

b 3 marks

c 3 marks

d 3 marks

Total marks for this topic

Translating shapes

Checking your understanding

1 Translate these shapes.

a) 2 to the right and 3 down

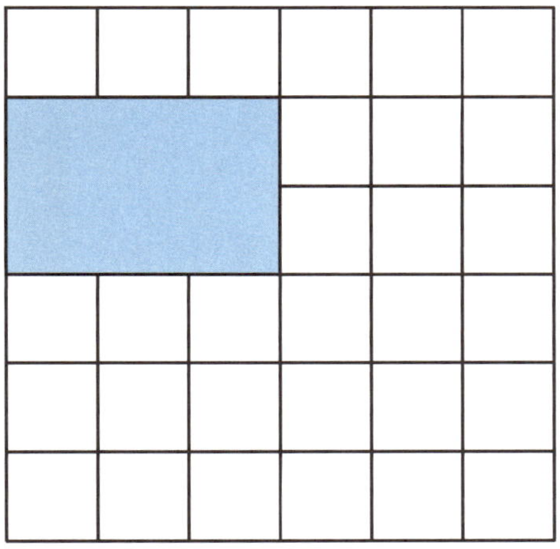

b) 1 to the left and 2 up

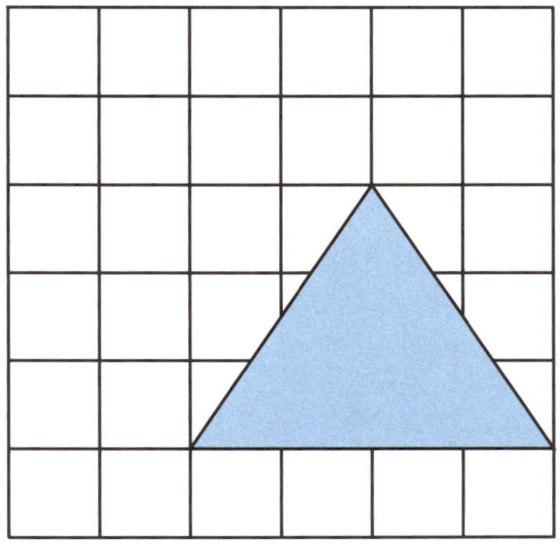

1 — 4 marks

2 Identify these translations.

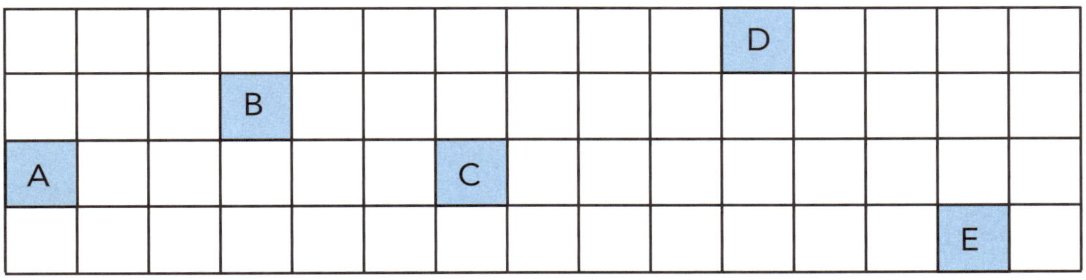

a) If you start at A and translate (6, 0) you land on ______. 2a — 1 mark

b) If you start on C and translate (−3, 1) you land on ______. 2b — 1 mark

c) The translation from D to B is ______. 2c — 1 mark

d) The translation from B to E is ______. 2d — 1 mark

e) The translation from A to D is ______. 2e — 1 mark

Total marks for this topic

Rotation about a point

Checking your understanding

1 Rotate these shapes 90° clockwise about point A.

a)
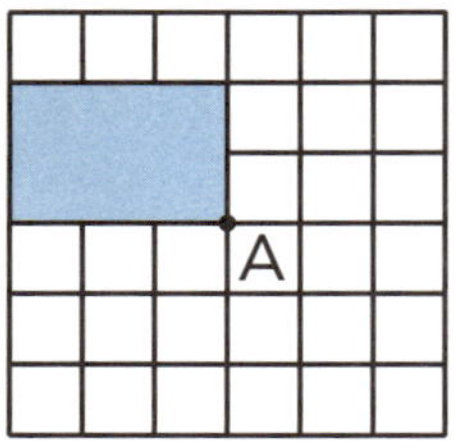

b)
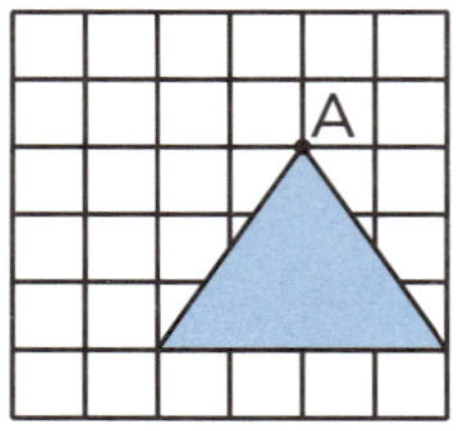

1a 2 marks

1b 2 marks

2 Rotate these shapes 180° anticlockwise about point B.

a)
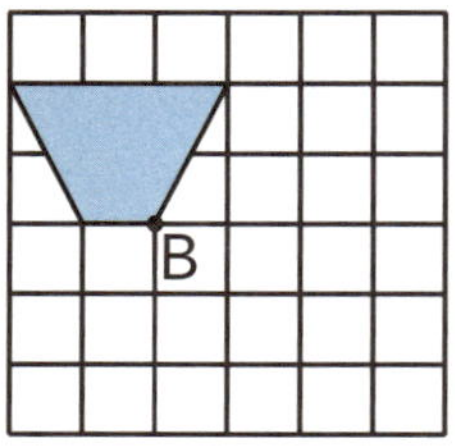

b)
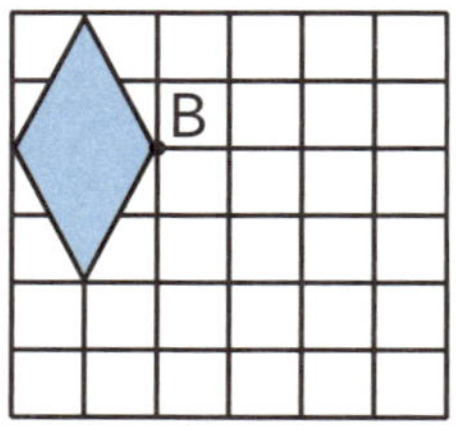

2a 2 marks

2b 2 marks

3 Rotate these shapes

a) 90° anticlockwise about C
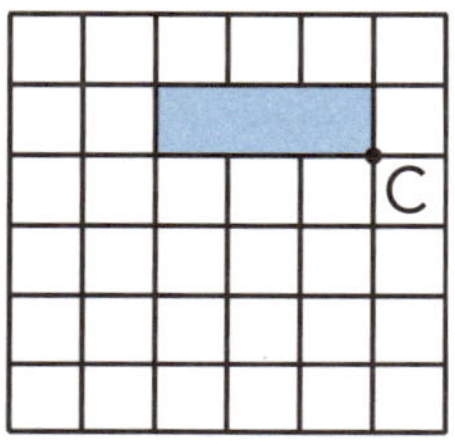

b) 180° clockwise about D
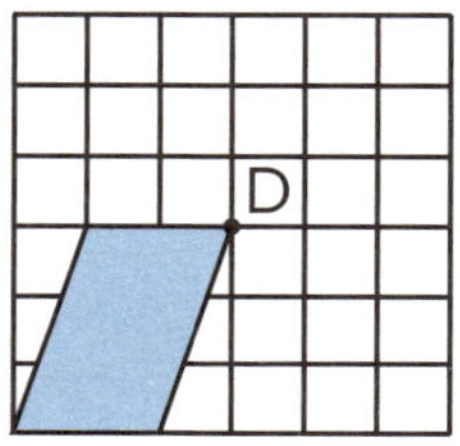

3a 2 marks

3b 2 marks

Using and applying

4 What rotation is needed to move the blue shape onto the white shape? Mark the point (centre) of rotation on the shape and give the direction and the number of degrees in the turn.

a)
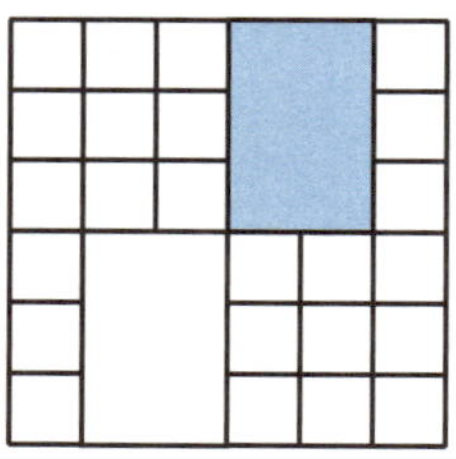

b)
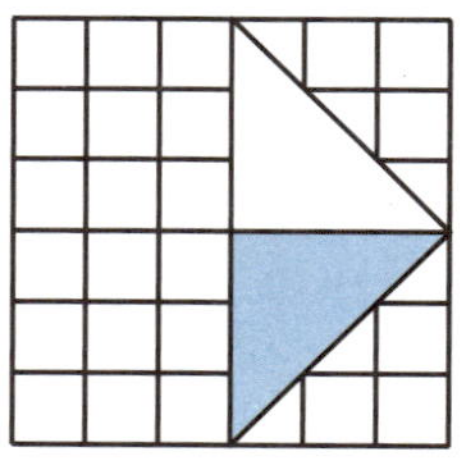

Direction =

Degrees of rotation =

Direction

Degrees of rotation

4a 2 marks

4b 2 marks

Total marks for this topic

Angles

Checking your understanding

1 Draw these angles.

a) 45°

b) 132°

1a — 2 marks

1b — 2 marks

2 Measure these angles to the nearest degree.

a)

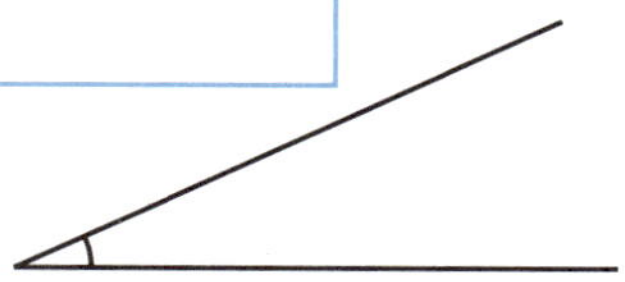

b)

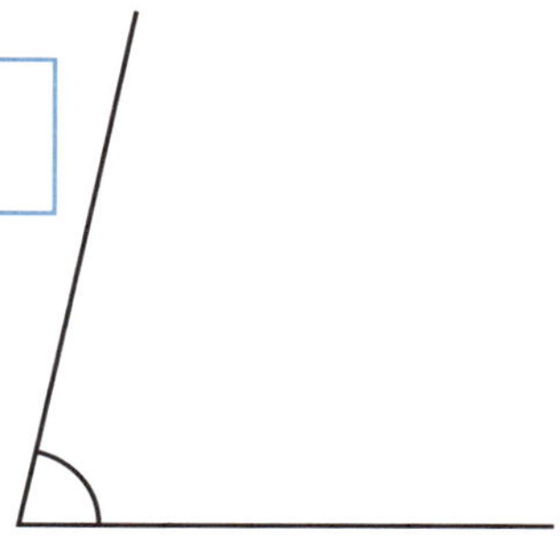

c)

d)

2a — 1 mark

2b — 1 mark

2c — 1 mark

2d — 1 mark

Using and applying

3

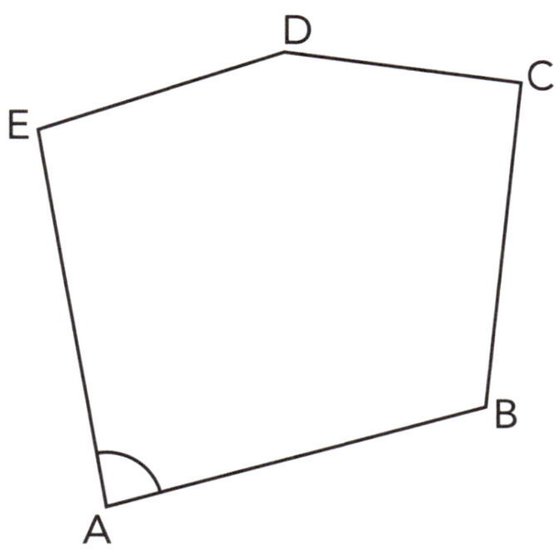

a) Measure angle A to the nearest degree.

b) Measure side BC to the nearest mm.

3a — 1 mark

3b — 1 mark

Total marks for this topic

Calculating angles

Checking your understanding

1 Calculate the unknown angles.

a) A = ☐

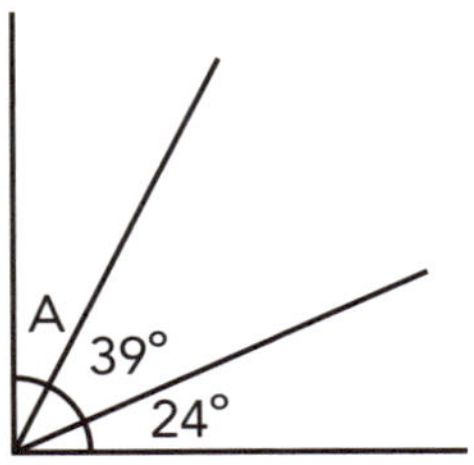

b) B = ☐

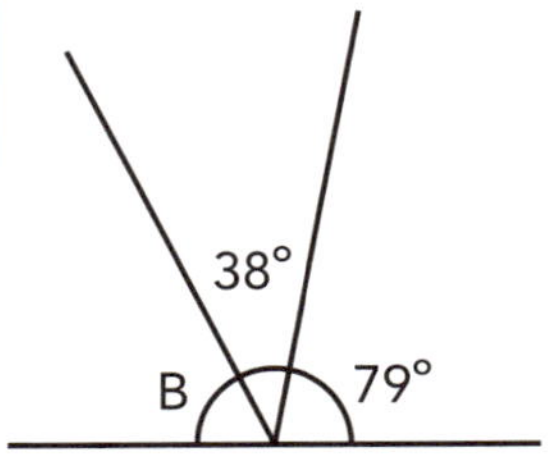

c) C = ☐

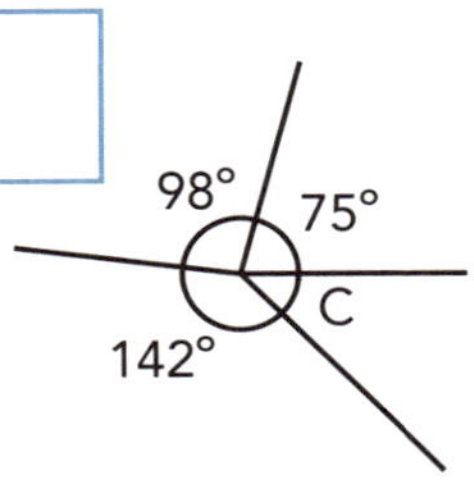

d) D = ☐

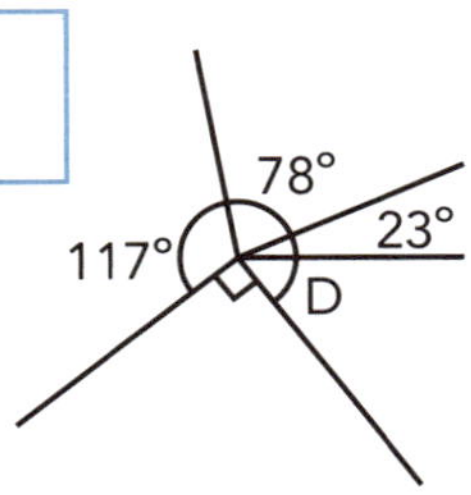

1a 1 mark

1b 1 mark

1c 1 mark

1d 1 mark

2 Calculate the unknown angles in these triangles.

a) A = ☐

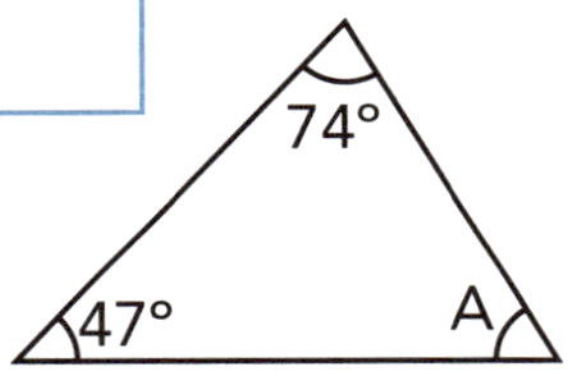

b) B = ☐

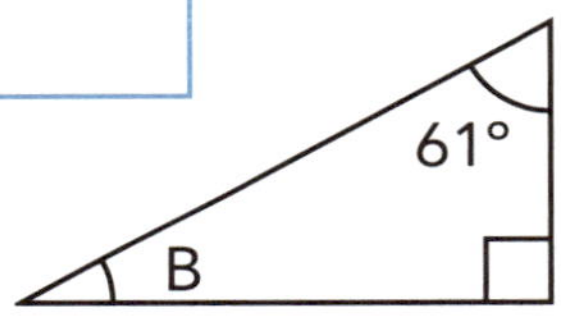

c) C = ☐

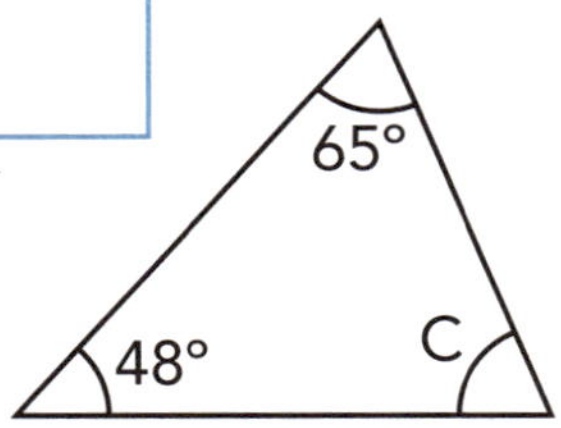

d) D = ☐

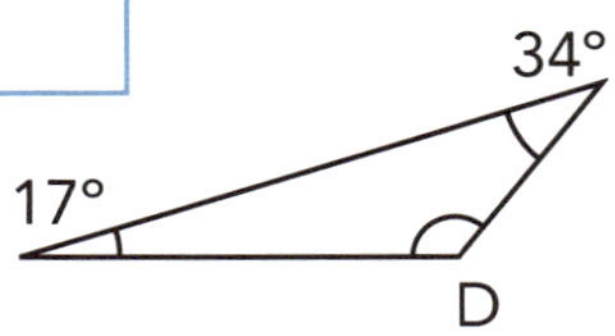

2a 1 mark

2b 1 mark

2c 1 mark

2d 1 mark

Using and applying

3 A ladder is leaned up against a vertical wall. The angle the ladder makes with the ground is 65°. What is the angle the ladder makes with the wall?

☐

3 1 mark

Angles at a point

1 A pizza is cut at the centre. Mum has a 60° piece, Dad has an 80° piece and 4 children share the rest equally. What is the size of the angle on each of their pieces?

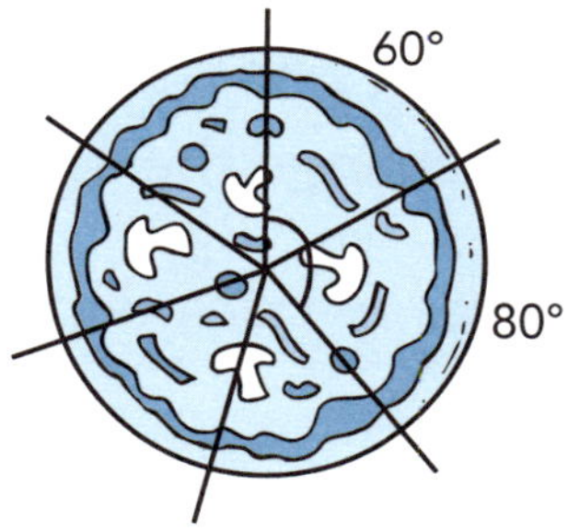

1 — 2 marks

2 A slice of cake is cut. The angle of the cut is 165°. How many 15° pieces can be cut from this piece?

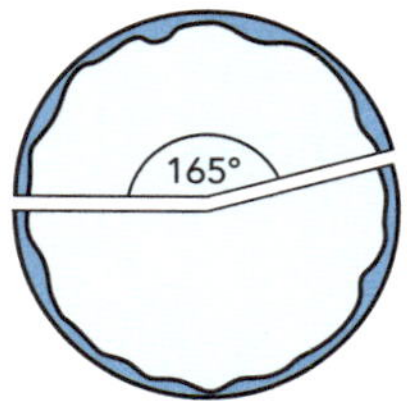

2 — 1 mark

3 James holds himself in front support position. The angle between his arms and his body is 72°. What is the angle between his legs and the floor?

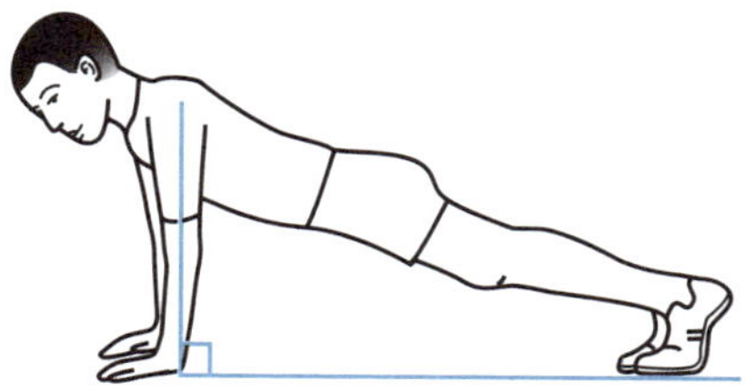

3 — 1 mark

4 Dami stands on a spot facing East in PE. She turns clockwise 123° and calls her new position P.

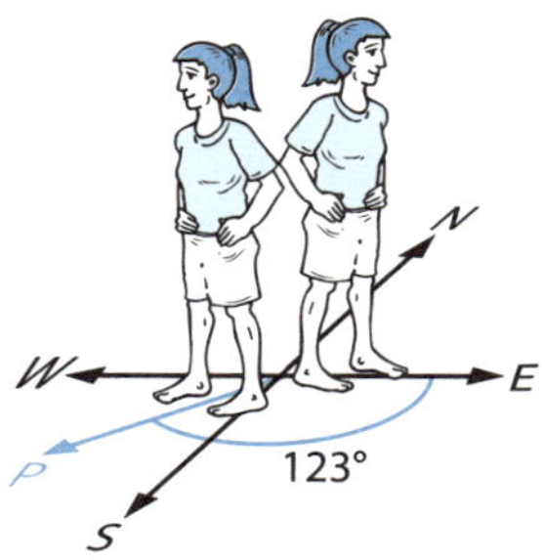

a) How far would she need to turn clockwise from P so that she is back in her starting position?

4a — 1 mark

b) How far would she need to turn anti-clockwise from P so that she is facing North?

4b — 1 mark

c) How far would she need to turn anti-clockwise from P to face South?

4c — 1 mark

Total marks for this topic

Units of measure

Checking your understanding

1 How do you change the following?

a) centimetres to decimetres

b) metres to kilometres

c) litres to millilitres

d) milligrams to centigrams

1 4 marks

2 Complete these statements.

a) 1 inch = ☐ cm **b)** 1 m = ☐ feet

c) 1 kg = ☐ lbs **d)** 1 foot = ☐ cm

e) 1 ounce = ☐ g **f)** 1 litre = ☐ pints

2 6 marks

3 Complete these calculations.

a) 325 m = ☐ km **b)** 4325 g = ☐ kg

c) ☐ m = 21 cm **d)** ☐ mm = 0.3 cm

e) 0.4 litres = ☐ cl **f)** 1.3 kg = ☐ dg

3 6 marks

4 Fill in the missing units.

a) 4.2 litres = 42 ☐ **b)** 40 cm = 400 ☐ **c)** 5000 cm = 50 ☐

d) 40 litres = 40,000 ☐ **e)** 5.3 kg = 530 ☐ **f)** 453.5 ☐ = 4.535 km

4 6 marks

Using and applying

5 To make a model castle, Cyla needs 14 cm strips of wood to put on the outside walls.

a) She buys wood in 2 m lengths. How many strips can she cut from each length she buys?

5a — 1 mark

b) Cyla needs 400 strips. What is the total length of wood on the model? Give your answer in metres.

5b — 1 mark

6 There are 74 children in Y6. Each child has a cup of orange juice. There are 125 ml of orange juice in each cup. Mr Wright buys orange juice in litre cartons. How many litres of orange juice does he need to buy?

6 — 2 marks

7 Which is better value: 6 kg of apples at £2.40 or 6 lb of apples at £1.40?

Explain your answer.

7 — 2 marks

8 Miguel travels 40 miles on his bike. How many kilometres is that?

8 — 1 mark

9 Shannon has 7.8 m of blue ribbon, 900 mm of red ribbon and 800 cm of green ribbon.

a) In which colour has she the longest length? Explain your answer.

9a — 2 marks

b) What is the total length of ribbon she has?

9b — 2 marks

Total marks for this topic

The area of a rectangle

Checking your understanding

1 Find the area of these rectangles.

a)

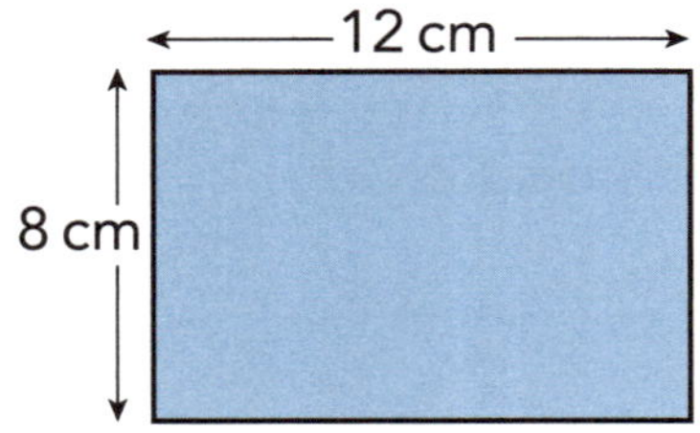

Working out:

Area =

1a 2 marks

b)

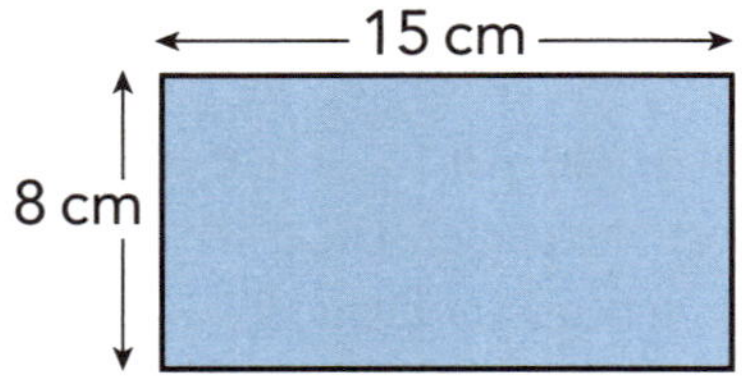

Working out:

Area =

1b 2 marks

c)

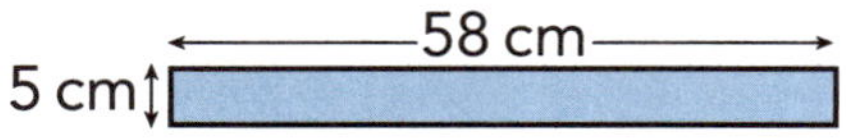

Working out:

Area =

1c 2 marks

d)

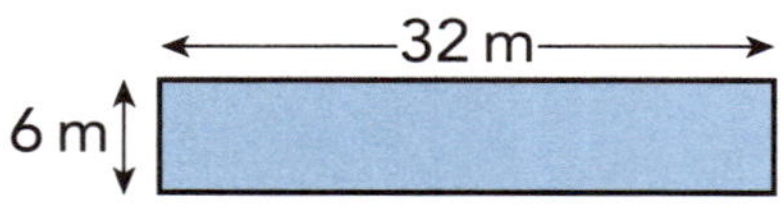

Working out:

Area =

1d 2 marks

Using and applying

2 These shapes are made of rectangles joined together. Calculate the total area of each shape.

a)

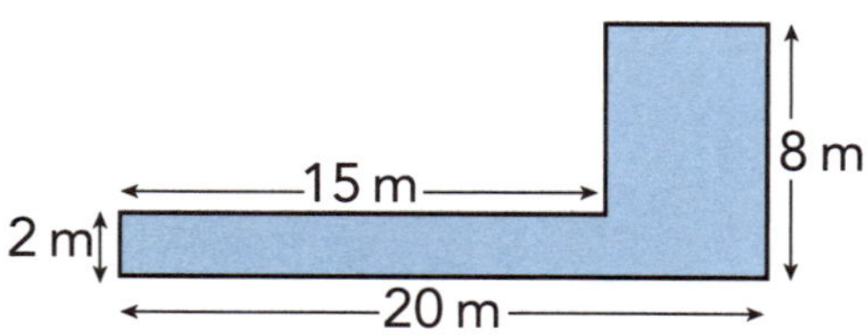

Working out:

Area =

2a 2 marks

b)

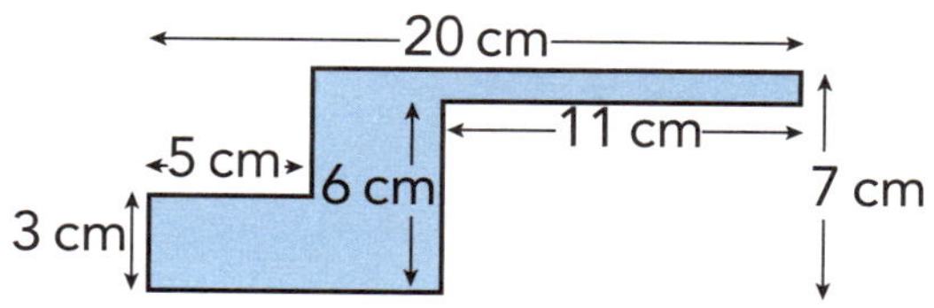

Working out:

Area =

2b
2 marks

3 A rectangle has an area of 60 cm^2. If one side has a length of 12 cm, what is the length of the other side?

3
2 marks

4 Tegan needs a piece of material 3 m by 18 m to make a dragon costume. What is the area of the material she needs?

4
2 marks

5 Cameron's bedroom measures 5.5 m by 8 m. Cameron chooses a carpet for it that costs £9 per m^2. What will the carpet for the room cost?

5
2 marks

6 Bartosz has a garden made of rectangles put together. What is the total area of his garden?

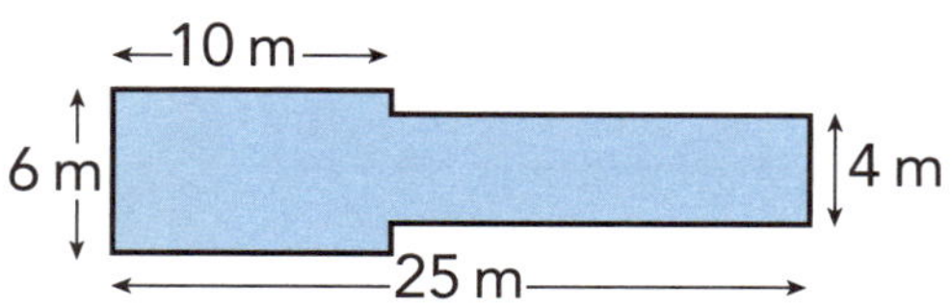

Show your working:

Area =

6
2 marks

Total marks for this topic

Finding the mean and median

Checking your understanding

1 Find the mean and median of these sets of numbers. Remember to show your working.

a) 5, 6, 5, 3, 1 mean = ☐ median = ☐ 1a 2 marks

b) 7, 2, 5, 2, 2, 1, 2 mean = ☐ median = ☐ 1b 2 marks

c) 6.2, 4.5, 8, 2.1, 4.2 mean = ☐ median = ☐ 1c 2 marks

Using and applying

2 Kadhi had five attempts at climbing a climbing wall. These are the heights he reached:

Attempt	1	2	3	4	5
Height reached (in metres)	3.6	5.9	9.6	3.6	6.3

Kadhi's mean height was ☐, his median was ☐,

his mode was ☐ and his range was ☐.

Show your working:

2 4 marks

3 Emma played 7 games of darts.
Her scores were 35, 28, 85, 82, 17, 82 and 105

Emma's mean score was ☐, her median was ☐,

her mode was ☐ and her range was ☐.

Show your working:

3 4 marks

Total marks for this topic ☐

Comparing two data sets

Checking your understanding

1 a) Find the mode, median, mean and range of data sets A and B.

A 15, 0, 14, 0, 1 **B** 2, 3, 7, 4, 7, 1, 11

mode = ☐ median = ☐ mode = ☐ median = ☐

range = ☐ mean = ☐ range = ☐ mean = ☐

1a 8 marks

b) Data set ☐ has a higher range and data set ☐ has a higher mode.

1b 2 marks

Using and applying

2 Josh counts the number of children that play with the stilts and the number that play with the space hoppers each day for a week. He writes down his findings.

Stilts	24	16	32	18	10
Space hoppers	33	22	24	15	11

Compare how much the two types of equipment are played with using the mean and median.

2 6 marks

3 The TopX and King groups in the chess club write down their ages.

TopX	9	10	8	11	11	8	7	10	10
King	7	9	7	9	10	11	11	9	8

Use the mode and range to compare the data from the two groups.

3 6 marks

Which group has a higher average age?

Total marks for this topic

Conversion graphs

Checking your understanding

a)

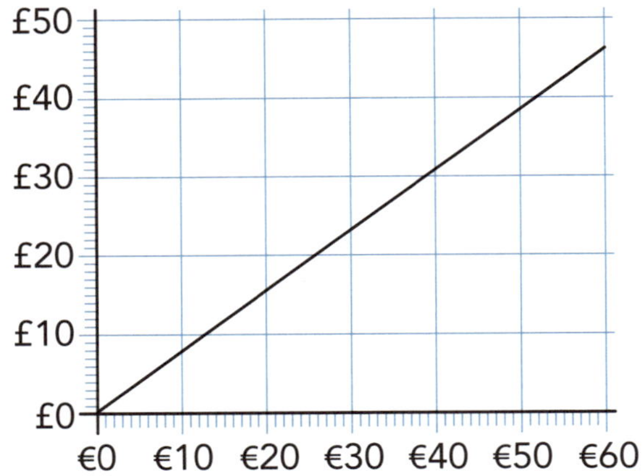

Complete these price tags.

i) £1 = €

ii) £5 = €

iii) ☐ 20 = ☐ 26

a — 3 marks

Using and applying

b) A jacket costs £45. Use the conversion graph to work out how many euros it would cost.

b — 1 mark

c) Christian buys an MP3 player for £24 and sells it for €28.

Does he make a profit? YES NO

Use the conversion graph to help you explain your answer.

c — 2 marks

d) Jacques pays £80 for €120. He sells the euros to a friend at the exchange rate shown on the conversion graph above. How many pounds does he make?

d — 2 marks

e) The price of a computer game, Dare2, falls from £20 to £17. Use the conversion graph to work out the approximate price change in euros.

e — 2 marks

Total marks for this topic

Pie charts

Checking your understanding

1

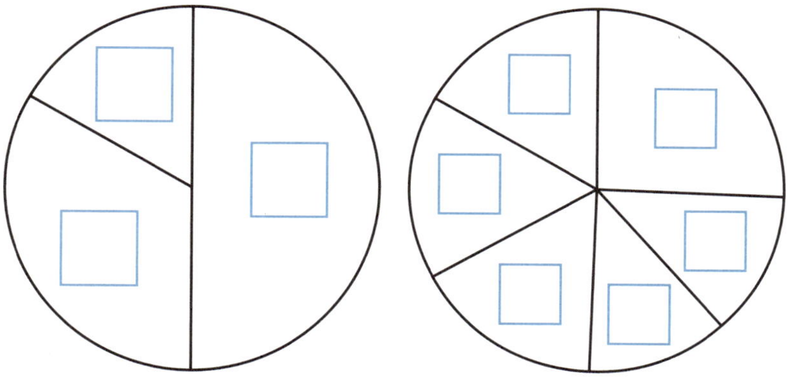

a) Label the fractions that show the size of the sections on these pie charts.

1a — 6 marks

b) Colour the section that shows a proportion of 12.5%.

1b — 1 mark

Using and applying

2 There are 36 children in Hannah's class. There are 20 children in Sam's class. They each ask the children in their class how long they spent watching TV last night.

Hannah's class

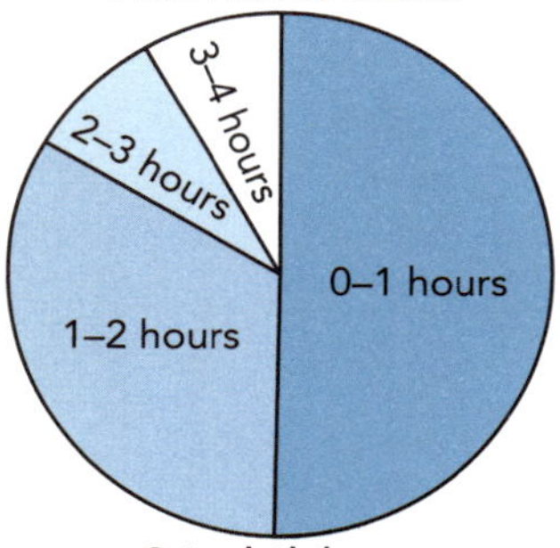

36 children

Sam's class

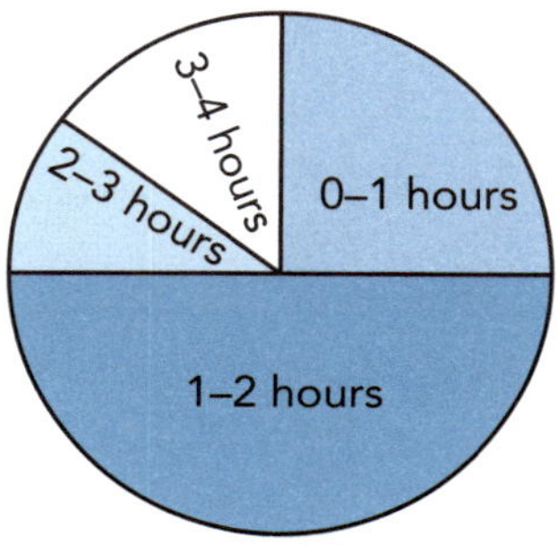

20 children

a) How many children in Sam's class watched TV for 0–1 hours?

2a — 1 mark

b) What fraction of Hannah's class watched for 3–4 hours?

2b — 1 mark

c) What % of Hannah's class watched the TV for 0–1 hours?

2c — 1 mark

d) ☐ % of children in Sam's class watched TV for 2–3 hours.

2d — 1 mark

e) In which class did more children watch TV for 1–2 hours?

Explain your answer.

2e — 2 marks

Total marks for this topic

Probability

Checking your understanding

1 Join these events to the correct letters on the probability scale.

It will get dark tonight.	It will snow in January.	If I toss a coin, I will get a head.

impossible — even — certain

A B C D E F

I will grow an extra leg tonight.	When I throw a die I will get a 5 or a 6.	One day, I will go to the moon.

1 2 marks

2 India tosses a fair coin 3 times.
She gets a head each time.

Now I've had three heads, I must get tails next time.

Is she correct? YES NO

Explain your answer.

2 1 mark

Using and applying

3 Yin Wai throws a fair die.

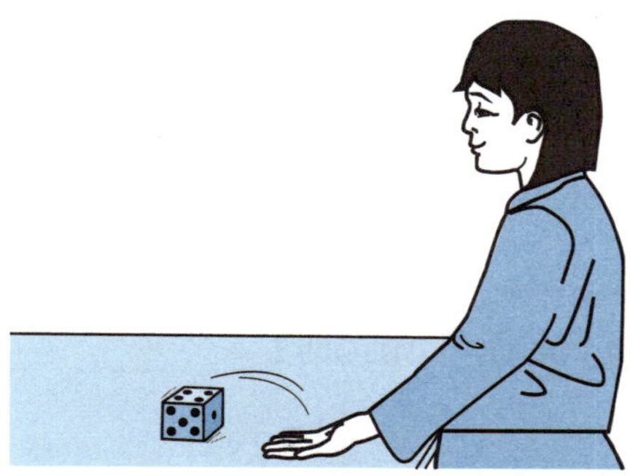

What is the probability of throwing the following?

a) 1

b) 6

c) an even number

d) 7

3a 1 mark

3b 1 mark

3c 1 mark

3d 1 mark

4 Joe puts 10 balls in a bag.

He picks one out at random.

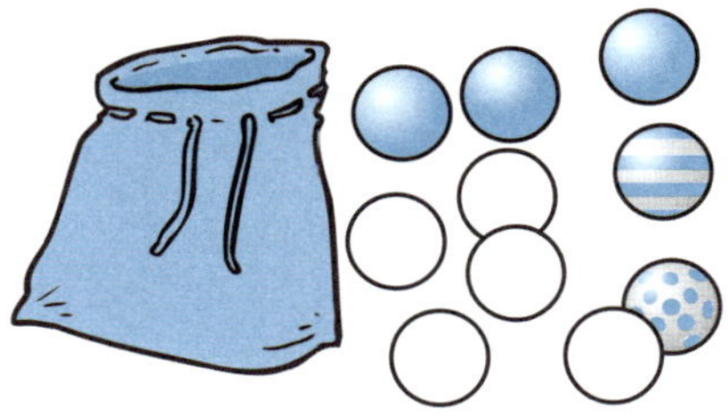

What is the probability that he picks the following?

a) a plain blue ball ☐ **b)** a plain white ball ☐

c) a spotty or white ball ☐ **d)** a red ball ☐

4a 1 mark

4b 1 mark

4c 1 mark

4d 1 mark

5 A vending machine has 20 slots to hold drinks bottles. Emma is blindfolded and pushes a button at random.

a) The probability of getting a bottle of still water is $\frac{1}{2}$. How many of the slots hold bottles of still water?

5a 1 mark

b) 5 slots hold fizzy water. What is the probability that Emma selects fizzy water?

5b 1 mark

c) The probability she selects a cola is $\frac{1}{10}$. How many slots hold cola?

5c 1 mark

d) The probability that Emma selects orange juice or apple juice is $\frac{3}{20}$. Write down all the combinations there are for the number of bottles of orange juice and the number of bottles of apple juice.

5d 2 marks

6 When Reuben reaches the traffic lights there is a 5/8 probability that the lights are red. What is the probability that they are not red?

6 1 mark

Total marks for this topic

Simple formulae

Checking your understanding

1 Find the value of the letters in these equations.

a) $A + 3 = 5$ $A =$ 1a 1 mark

b) $7 - B = 1$ $B =$ 1b 1 mark

c) $3 \times C = 15$ $C =$ 1c 1 mark

d) $D \div 2 = 26$ $D =$ 1d 1 mark

2 Circle the formula that shows the answer (A) you get when you divide a number (N) by 8, and then subtract 4.

$A = 4 - (N \div 8)$ $A = (8 \div N) - 4$

$A = 4 - (N \div 8)$ $A = (N \div 8) - 4$

2 1 mark

3 Write the formula where the answer (A) is found by adding 3 to a number (N) and then multiplying it by 6.

3 1 mark

Using and applying

4 The number of hours spent go-karting can be found by dividing the total cost by the price per hour of go-karting.

a) Using H for hours, T for total cost and P for price per hour, write a formula for the number of hours spent go-karting.

4a 1 mark

b) If go-karting costs £5 an hour, change the formula so it includes this information.

4b 1 mark

5 The total cost (T) of a class trip to the climbing wall is the number of pupils (P) multiplied by the entrance fee (E) plus the cost of the coach (C).

a) Write the formula for the total cost of the trip.

5a 1 mark

b) If the entrance fee is £3, the coach costs £150 and 25 pupils are in the class, what is the total cost of the trip?

5b 1 mark

6 The distance (D) that Billy runs can be worked out by multiplying the speed (S) at which he runs by the time (T) he runs.

a) Write the formula for the distance Billy runs.

6a 1 mark

b) Billy runs at a speed of 3.6 metres a second for 8 seconds. Write these numbers into the formula and calculate the distance Billy runs.

6b 1 mark

c) Write the formula if Billy runs 22 m in 4 seconds.

6c 1 mark

7 $A + B - C = 40$

A is double B and C is half of A. What are the values of A, B and C?

7 2 marks

8 $D \times E = 300$

D is three times E. What are the values of D and E?

8 2 marks

Total marks for this topic

Solving problems

Using and applying

1 Aadi wants to juggle 3 balls for 1 minute. If 3 in every 5 attempts are successful, how many goes does he need to have before he has been unsuccessful 10 times?

1

2 marks

2 A set of 5 numbers has a range of 7, a mean of 6, a mode of 3 and a median of 5.

Write the set of numbers.

2

2 marks

3 Mr Brown has a class of 35 pupils. Of the 27 children who have passed the Cycling Proficiency Test, 21 come to school on a bike. 10 children in the class do not come to school on a bike.

Use this information to complete the Carroll diagram.

	Comes to school on a bike.	Does not come to school on a bike.
Passed the Cycling Proficiency Test.		
Not passed the Cycling Proficiency Test.		

3

2 marks

4 Ami buys a new bike for £286 and a reflective jacket for £16. If the price includes 15% tax for each item, what is the total amount of tax she has to pay?

4

2 marks

5 Harry goes out on his scrambler bike. He has a radio unit so that he can keep in touch with base station. His distance from the base station during the day is shown on the graph.

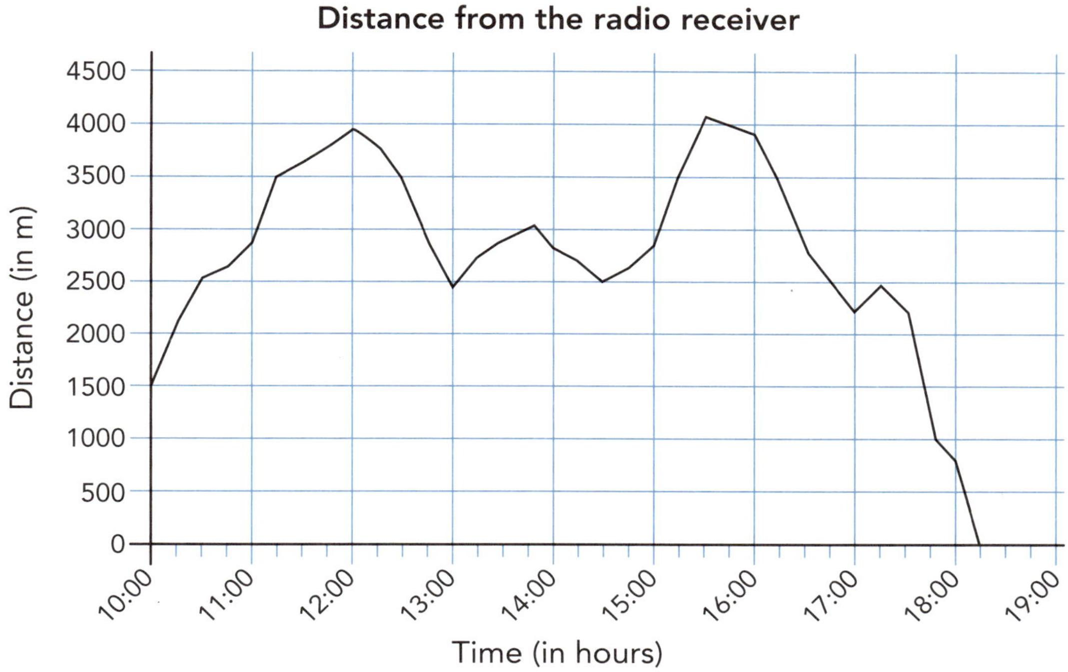

a) What is the greatest distance Harry goes from the base station?

5a — 1 mark

b) At what time is he 1000 m from the base station?

5b — 1 mark

c) The radio will not receive a signal when it is more than 3500 m from the base station. What is the total amount of time that Harry was out of range of the base station during the afternoon?

5c — 2 marks

6 Buxworth School is setting up a new football pitch. The football pitch is 90 m by 50 m. A bag of grass seed costs £4 and will cover 15 m^2. What would be the cost of putting grass seed over the entire pitch?

6 — 2 marks

Total marks for this topic

Solving number problems

Using and applying

1. Mrs Butcher gets out all the classroom equipment to reorganise it. There is equipment for maths, science and art. Each subject has three shelves for equipment. Altogether there are 72 pieces of equipment. How many pieces of equipment will go on each shelf if Mrs Butcher divides them equally?

1 2 marks

2. In the car park there are 5 cars for every 2 motorbikes. If there are 80 cars, how many motorbikes are there?

2 2 marks

3. Jacinta wants to go surfing. She pays £18 to hire a surfboard. She must share the surfing time equally with her brother. If it costs £1.20 to rent the board for 30 minutes, how much surfing time will Jacinta get?

3 2 marks

4. In a maths test there were 25 questions. Whitney didn't know the answer to 4 of the questions and was unsure about another 5 questions. What percentage of the test questions did Whitney know well?

4 2 marks

5 Michelle makes up party bags for her friends. In each bag she puts 3 sweets, 5 stickers and 2 pencils. When she had finished, she had used 75 stickers. How many sweets had she used?

5 2 marks

6 It costs £148 to go on a residential trip to Whitehall Outdoor Education Centre. There are two dining rooms. One has 8 tables and the other has 4 tables. The tables are all the same size. If Whitehall can accommodate 192 people, how many people can sit at each table?

6 2 marks

7 A theatre group visits a school. The school asks each pupil to contribute £1.25 to the cost of the group. 83 pupils contribute. The school has to pay £71.25 to make up the total cost of the group.

a) What was the cost of having the theatre group in school?

7a 2 marks

b) There are 136 pupils in the school. How much money would have been raised if they had all contributed as requested?

7b 2 marks

8 Mr Francomb asked everyone to collect sweet wrappers for a design project. India collected 18 different types of wrapper, but Leah collected four times as many. Leah presents her collection by sticking the wrappers on pieces of card. Each piece of card has the same number of wrappers on it. If she uses 12 pieces of card, how many wrappers are on each card?

8 2 marks

Total marks for this topic

Solving measure problems

Using and applying

1 Class 6 had Gunge Games as part of their leavers' celebrations. As part of the games, the pupils were squirting slimy foam at each other. Callum estimated that his can of slimy foam could squirt 28 m of foam. He divided the amount equally between the boys and the girls. If there were 4 girls he wanted to get, how many metres of slimy foam could he squirt on each girl?

1

2 marks

2 Dan has a recipe to make rice pudding for 4 people. Fill in the quantities he will need to make the same recipe for 6 people.

For 4 people	For 6 people
2 eggs	______ eggs
50 g butter	______ butter
800 ml milk	______ milk
100 g rice	______ rice
80 g sugar	______ sugar

2

5 marks

3 A bottle of lemonade can fill either 3 small tumblers and 2 large tumblers or 6 small tumblers and 1 large tumbler.

If a small tumbler holds 200 ml of lemonade, how much lemonade is there in the bottle?

3

2 marks

4 Cameron and his little sister Imogen together weigh the same as their dad. Cameron weighs twice as much as Imogen, and their dad weighs 4 stones more than Cameron. What do the three people weigh?

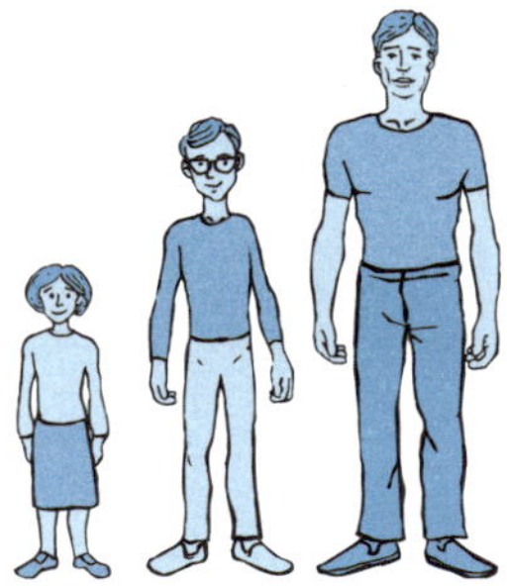

4 — 2 marks

5 Sol uses a timetable to work out which bus to catch when she is meeting some friends in town. Sol has to catch the bus at Norton.

Norton	07:20	07:50	08:15	08:35	09:00	09:25
Gleadless	07:31	08:01	08:26	08:46	09:11	09:36
Manor Top	07:36	08:06	08:31	08:51	09:16	09:42
Heeley	07:49	08:19	08:44	09:04	09:29	09:55
Bramhall Lane	07:59	08:29	08:54	09:14	09:39	10:05
City Centre	08:13	08:43	09:06	09:28	09:53	10:19

a) If Sol is meeting her friends in the city centre at quarter to ten, what time will she need to catch the bus at Norton?

5a — 1 mark

b) How long does it take the bus to get from Gleadless to the city centre?

5b — 2 marks

c) Sol's uncle gets on the bus at the Manor Top and gets off at Bramhall Lane. For what fraction of her journey is her uncle on the bus?

5c — 2 marks

d) There is a football match at Bramhall Lane and the traffic makes the bus 17 minutes late. How long does it take Sol to get from Norton to the City Centre?

5d — 2 marks

Total marks for this topic

Solving shape and space problems

Using and applying

1 A shape is made from four identical rectangles. The rectangles measure 8 cm by 3 cm.

a) Calculate the perimeter of the shape.

1a — 2 marks

b) Calculate the total area of the shape.

1b — 2 marks

2

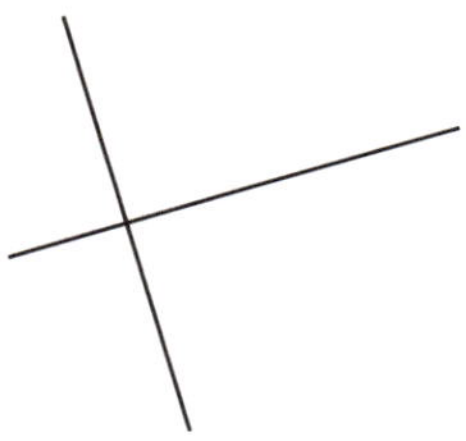

These are the diagonals of a shape.

Name the shape.

2 — 1 mark

3 Three identical circles fit exactly into a rectangle. The radius of each circle is 6 m.

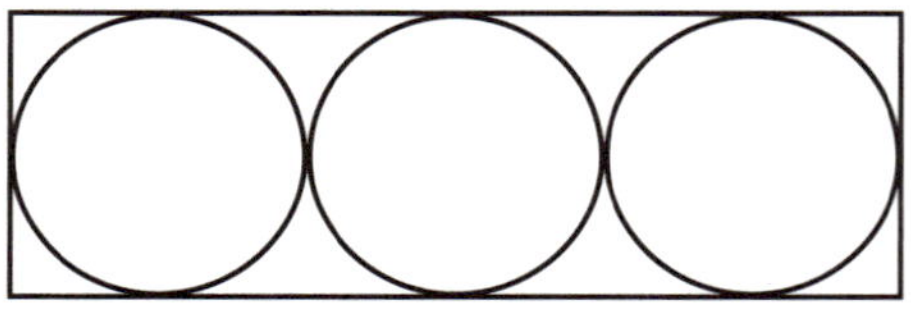

a) What is the perimeter of the rectangle?

3a — 2 marks

b) What is the area of the rectangle?

3b — 2 marks

4 Caitlin is constructing a honeycomb in science and tessellates some regular hexagons.

a) Calculate the size of angle A.

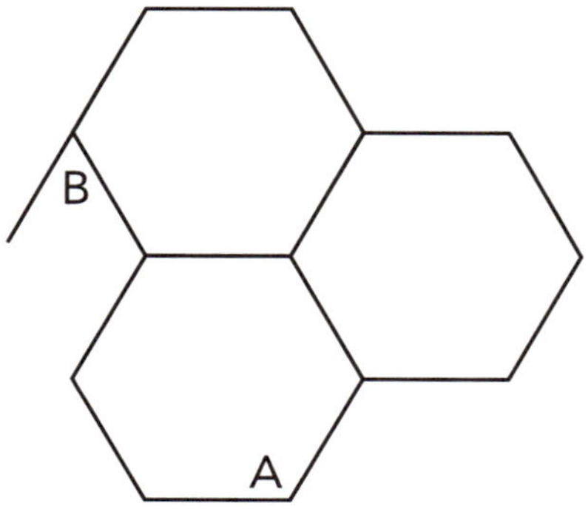

4a — 2 marks

b) Calculate the size of angle B.

4b — 2 marks

5 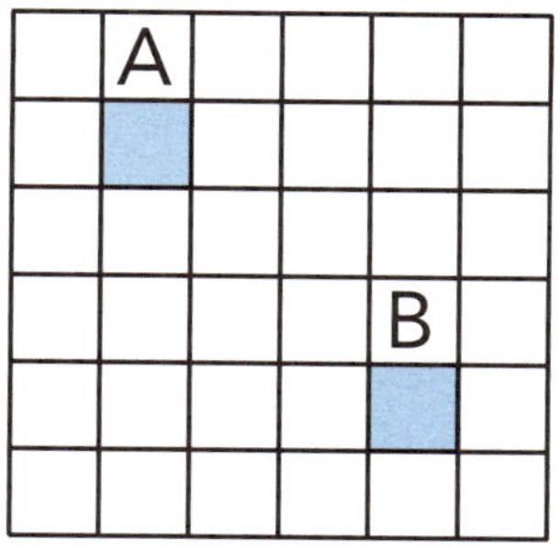

A grid has two squares coloured – square A and square B. James and Ben investigate how to move square A on to square B. James says B is a translation of A and Ben says it is a reflection of A.

a) Who is correct?

5a 1 mark

b) Explain your answer.

5b 2 marks

6 John designs a logo for Hilltop School that is a blue triangle on a white background. The white background is a square with a side length of 6 cm. What is the area of the blue triangle?

6 2 marks

7 A construction block for the school playground is made by sticking four identical rectangles together. Each rectangle has a width of 15 cm.

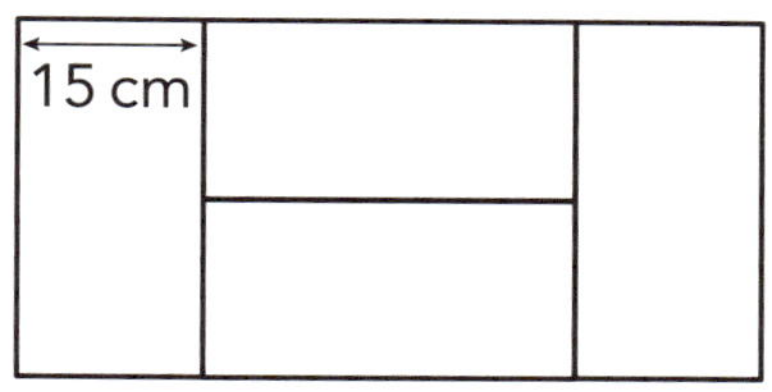

a) What is the length of each block?

7a 2 marks

b) What is the area of each block?

7b 2 marks

8 Yin Wai has a cube with a side length of 5 cm.

a) Calculate the surface area of the cube.

8a 2 marks

b) Calculate the volume of the cube.

8b 2 marks

Total marks for this topic

Key facts

Counting and understanding number

Place value

- Each number is made up of digits. The position of the digit in a number gives it its value.

Hundreds	Tens	Units	tenths	hundredths	
7	8	4	3	5	
= 700 +	80 +	4 +	$\frac{3}{10}$ +	$\frac{5}{100}$ =	784.35

Rounding

- When rounding, remember that 5 goes up! 6.785 = 6.79

Negative numbers

- Integers are just whole numbers.
- When counting from negative up to positive or from positive down to negative, **remember to count 0!**
- When counting on a number line, count to the right when adding and to the left when subtracting.

Fractions

- The numerator tells you how many equal parts are used.
- The denominator tells you how many equal parts there are.

Reducing a fraction to its simplest form

- If you are asked to find a proportion or ratio of two things or numbers you are being asked to find a fraction (in its lowest form).

Fraction, decimal and percentage equivalents

- Remember as many of these as you can.

Fraction	$\frac{1}{2}$	$\frac{1}{10}$	$\frac{1}{4}$	$\frac{3}{4}$	Nearly $\frac{1}{3}$
Decimal	0.5	0.1	0.25	0.75	0.33
Percentage	50%	10%	25%	75%	33%

The vocabulary of ratio and proportion

- Ratio is 'to every'.
- Proportion is 'in every'.
- Reduce ratios and proportions to their lowest form.

Knowing and using number facts

- **Tables:** it is essential that you know these really well.
- **Squares:** numbers made when another number is multiplied by itself.
- **Multiples:** numbers that have been multiplied by a given number.
- **Factors:** numbers that can divide into a given number without leaving a remainder.

Checking your answers

- Inverse means opposite!
- Check addition by subtraction – and vice versa.
- Check division by multiplication – and vice versa.
- Use 'friendly numbers' when estimating: 2, 5, 10 etc.

Calculating

- Multiplying numbers by 10 and 100: Push the digits to the left once for × 10 and twice for ÷ 100.
- Dividing numbers by 10 and 100: Push the digits to the right once for ÷ 10 and twice for ÷ 100.
- Addition and subtraction of decimals:
  1. Line up the decimal points when you write out the sum.
  2. Fill empty places with a 0.
  3. Remember to put the decimal point in your answer!
- Multiplication and division of decimals:
  1. × and ÷ are opposites.
  2. Remember – there must be the same number of digits after the decimal point in the answer as there are in the question.

Brackets

- Always do the brackets in equations first.

Choosing your method

- Remember to look at the numbers you are working with. You might be able to use a good mental strategy rather than a written method, or it might be best to use a calculator.

Understanding shape

3-D shapes

- Vertices are corners.
- Faces are flat surfaces.
- Edges are edges!